What Next, Doctor Peck?

By the same author

ALL ABOUT MEN

WHAT NEXT, DOCTOR PECK?

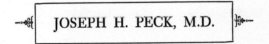

JOSEPH H. PECK, M.D.

Prentice-Hall, Inc.

Englewood Cliffs, N. J.

Second printing ...... September, 1959

To Ruth

Preface

Deep Creek Country lies along the western border of the State of Utah. Briefly, it includes everything in a fifty-mile-wide strip of territory running south about one hundred miles from Wendover to the Deep Creek Mountains. The Indians call the region Ibapah.

Forty-odd years ago this was an isolated pocket of the Old West. Because of that isolation it was unspoiled by most of the faults of our American culture of the period, and endowed by most of the good qualities. In it there was no evidence of law and order except as such were practiced by the fifteen hundred or so residents themselves. There were no churches or men of the cloth to guide faltering footsteps, no income taxes, and no conception of the meaning of the word conformity.

In this Eden people married, raised families, played and quarreled like human beings any place else, and died. They made their own amusements, settled their differences without benefit of jurisprudence, and spent precious little time thinking about the state of the world in general or worrying about the future of the human race.

The land itself lived up to the early pronouncements of Washington statesmen as being worthless for anything but the propagation of coyotes, rattlesnakes and lizards. It was well populated by these creatures, by wild horses and sage hens, and by thousands of ducks and mosquitoes in the brackish swamp lands along the shores of what had once been an enormous lake known as Bonneville.

Over half the land was as flat as a billiard table and was covered with a layer of salt averaging three feet in thickness. This, of course, was barren of any kind of natural growth, either vegetable or animal. Of the rest, twenty square miles was swamp; ten, fertile valley land; a thousand, hills and valleys covered with shad scale and desert juniper. A lofty mountain range that sported real trees made the southern boundary.

When I was a young and inexperienced physician I spent two very happy years there in Ibapah as the sole representative of my own and kindred professions. In these years I gained a wholesome respect for the dignity of man regardless of his color or his position on life's ladder, and for his ability to live at peace with his neighbors when he was not contaminated by the avarice and greed which grow, along with education and social progress, in more thickly settled and sophisticated communities.

My patients, friends and neighbors included practitioners of the oldest profession and their male parasites; bums from the skid rows of Salt Lake City and Sacramento; the construction personnel of a world-famous company; prospectors and small shopkeepers who were veterans of boom camps from Tombstone, Arizona, to Goldfield, Nevada; ranchers and their farm hands, generally classed as cowboys and sheepherders; and a very primitive tribe of Indians. It was a human Noah's Ark.

Nine months of the year our only connection with the civilized world was one transcontinental railway, the Western Pacific, which crossed the north end of the area. What with the primitive state of transportation and the lack of anything that could be classed as a road, the distances between habitations were appalling. A tiny settlement of hardy pioneers existed wherever there was a trickle of water from the surrounding mountains; at Gold Hill, the metropolis of the region, there was no water fit to drink within twenty-five miles.

Due to the fact that next-door Nevada was a "wet" state and within walking distance of most of the area, other liquids were not so scarce.

We had a choice of bottled goods to take the place of the scanty supply of water, and we also had plenty of navy beans, dried fruits, and canned goods. Groceries were shipped by rail from Salt Lake City to Wendover, and then to Gold Hill by wagon or, later, by truck.

Nobody was rich, nobody destitute. There were no aged or sufferers from chronic illnesses. Homes were tents or jerry-built cabins. There was one telephone line between Wendover and Gold Hill. No picture shows, radio or television; no swimming pools and no mortgages. Few automobiles and no auto wrecks. Never was a shot fired in anger, and in Gold Hill there was no necessity for setting aside any valuable real estate as a graveyard.

It was a Utopia of sorts in what was a hell of a country for everyone but the Indians. They put up with it in a dignified and tolerant manner, and believed that the white race were all lunatics and to be pitied.

Such diversions as a plague of rattlesnakes and rabid coyotes kept life from settling into a monotonous routine. And there were plenty of incidents involving human beings to give considerable variety to life there. All the standard characters of a typical western made their entrances and their exits. But because the drama was for real, most of them fell flat on their faces before they reached the wings.

Only a handful of the white settlers, the Indians and the wild horses maintained the dignity with which God endows all his creations.

I intend to tell a true story of these happenings. They all occurred pretty much as I shall record them, but I have

taken an author's license to mix things up in such a way
that the more asinine antics of my contemporaries there
will not be too easily recognized. Some of them may still
be around and might wish to forget their youthful pranks.
If this were not the case, I could let my imagination run
and color the tale to conform more closely to pictures of
old mining camps painted by less inhibited writers. But I
would hate to be called a liar by my old friends.

—JOSEPH H. PECK

Contents

What Next, Doctor Peck?

The Wendover Car

One bitter cold November night in 1916 my feelings about the practice of medicine in a central Utah town were just about as warm as the wind that whistled outside my window. There is no despair equal to that of a young doctor when he has first hung out his shingle and offered his services to an indifferent public.

The telephone rang. I didn't waste any time at all in answering it. The practice I was expecting to appear was being most deliberate in its coming.

"Dr. Joseph Peck?" Central said. "Salt Lake City is calling."

My heart sank even further. The chances of my being called from Gunnison, in San Pete County, all 150 miles into the metropolis to tend a patient were small indeed.

"Here's your party," Central said. And then I was talking to the Chief Surgeon of the Western Pacific Railway.

"I wonder," he said, "if I could persuade you to give up your practice . . ."

Practice? I wondered if maybe he'd got the wrong party.

". . . and take a contract with the Utah Construction Company. It should net you at least a thousand dollars a month."

At that time the average income of physicians in Utah was three thousand dollars a *year*.

"Yes, doctor," I said. "I'll be in Salt Lake City tomorrow morning for instructions."

3

It did not occur to me then to ask him how or where I was to come into this fortune. I didn't much care.

Money was a commodity I had not been much used to. I had worked my way through medical college as a telegraph operator for the Chicago, Burlington & Quincy Railroad back in Missouri, where I'd been born thirty-one years before that November night. My internship in St. Mark's Hospital in Salt Lake City had just been completed the previous spring. The money I had saved from relieving doctors in the coal camps of the Utah Fuel Company and the copper mines at Bingham Canyon was about used up. I was still burdened with medical school debts.

Because of the extent of my practice I thought it necessary to awaken only two people to announce my departure: my girl friend, and the livery stable proprietor, who also ran the town's only gasoline pump.

Driving all that night to Salt Lake City, still unaware of precisely what the future held for me, I relapsed into despair. Like any other young doctor I was doubtful of my bedside manner, and I fully realized how poorly I was equipped. I was also well aware of how little the medical profession knew then about the diseases which afflict humanity.

The interview next morning did not do much more than give me the facts. The Western Pacific was building a branch line southward from Wendover, Utah, to a new copper camp some place out in the Great Salt Lake Desert. It needed a doctor to look after the construction workers.

"We've had two men on the job," the Chief Surgeon told me, "and they were more experienced than you. But both of them blew up within a week."

I gulped.

"It's up to you," he continued, "to prove you can take it."

I asked a few questions about the region to which, it began to look, I was being exiled.

"You may find," he said, "the moral tone a cut below the pious atmosphere of Utah. Wendover is on the Nevada line. There'll be plenty of female companionship, but only on a cash-on-delivery basis."

He had heard, he added, that there wasn't a decent white female within fifty miles of the place I was headed for who was not married or too young to think about boys.

It was obviously going to be a place usually described in the movies of the time as "out where the West begins." I decided I had better assume the plumage which according to Hollywood was worn by all "real men" there.

I discarded my doctor's sober garb and substituted a mackinaw coat of dark green and black plaid, corduroy trousers that laced about the calves of my legs and stopped the circulation below that point, and high laced boots. I turned down the tops of my dark green socks over these for a tasteful trimming.

I had looked up two other recent ex-interns, and they came to the railroad station with their nurse girl friends to bid me *bon voyage*. The girls said I looked cute, just like the hero who always rescued Pearl White in *The Perils of Pauline,* a popular suspense-thriller movie serial of the time.

I could not honestly return the compliment, for Miss White had the prettiest ankles in the business. That was all the movie queens dared expose for the camera in those days, but we boys were endowed with active imaginations.

The starving ex-interns shook their heads and deplored the fact that I would give up the hallowed traditions of general practice for mere money.

Twenty-four hours after that telephone call from the Chief Surgeon, my train to the West was called. I took a lingering look at the nurses and hurried out of the waiting room, anxious to begin my role in this saga of man, woman and nature in the rough.

On the platform it was spitting snow. The wind blew the

icy grains against my face so hard it felt like a sand blast as I walked to the Wendover car at the rear of the train.

I found a couple of paddy wagons parked at the steps of the Wendover car. Policemen were carrying men inside as if they were loading a refrigerator car with sides of beef. From the looks of this cargo I thought the air would be better on the open platform of the car for as long as I could stand the snow and the cold. Also, I did not want to start this great adventure with an honor guard of Salt Lake City's finest.

I waited in the shadows until the police were finished and gone. Meanwhile I surveyed the car itself. It was already a museum piece. Made of wood and painted a sickly green to match the steel Pullmans up ahead, it was built high off the trucks. An iron stove pipe that stuck out of the roof was belching black coal smoke at a lively rate.

Within a year this relic would become the entire passenger rolling stock of the Deep Creek Railway. Its last resting place, I have heard, was the campus of the University of California as a shrine to the good old days.

Not long after the train left the sheds, I was freezing. I took a last deep breath of clean air and went inside.

Here the antique motif was even more marked. In one corner a big old-fashioned coal stove was bolted to the floor and half surrounded by a sheet iron shield to keep it from scorching the woodwork. Facing the open side of the stove were little red plush seats, their backs black and shiny from the thousands of restless, greasy heads that had rubbed against them over the years.

The windows were single paned, instead of double paned as in most passenger cars, and so were covered over with frost from the conflict of the warm moist atmosphere on the inside (the upper half of the stove was red hot) and the cold dry air outside. As the car swayed from side to side, each of these windows rattled in a different key.

Half a dozen gas jets hanging from the roof provided what little illumination the car had. Their feeble glow turned the blue walls into a nauseous hue.

The floor was covered with well-worn linoleum plentifully stained with tobacco juice, especially around the spittoons by each seat. If one of these spittoons was accidentally kicked hard, it gave forth an odor that, when blended with the stench of stale beer and unwashed bodies, was indescribable.

On either side of the middle of the car, and above the windows, were two large, glass-fronted cases, each of which contained a big saw, a little saw, and a wicked-looking axe. Gilt letters on the glass instructed: "To Use, Break Glass."

The use for these weapons was left to the imagination of the individual passenger. Was it to repel train robbers? To subdue a general fight? Or to remodel the wretched vehicle into a chicken coop? Certainly tools would have been unnecessary in the event of a wreck, for a child could have kicked his way out of the thing.

It was evident that the Western Pacific Railway placed no high value on its Wendover business. Looking over the present cargo, I could not blame it. Ten feet around the stove, seats and floor were covered with specimens of masculine humanity sprawled over and under one another in such a way that no man could be sure whose ankle he would be scratching should the occasion arise. It seemed likely that it would arise, for each man must have been transporting quite a menagerie upon his person.

I had no wish to acquire a nest of seam-squirrels in my fine new clothes, and decided to return to the platform and freeze.

Then a female voice sang out from the shadows in the back of the car. "Come on back here with us, Doc. You'll stand less danger of getting crummy."

As best I could, I picked my way through the men on the

floor toward the direction of the voice. Finally I reached the distaff side of the party.

The speaker I discovered to be a large and commanding female whose entire appearance advertised that she was a madam. In the two seats behind her were four recruits for her army of workers in the vineyard. Once upon a time these may have been white slaves, but if they still aspired to that classification they would have had to be put down as third-class scullery maids.

If followed for many years, the oldest profession is harder on women than the medical branch is on men.

Back there in the women's division of the car it was cold, but the troupe had pasted newspapers against the windows and sat wrapped in blankets and comforters as though they were on a sleigh ride.

"Before you sit down," the boss lady advised me, "you better get out your soogan."

I did not know quite what she meant. "I don't think I've got one," I said.

"Never mind," she said. "My robe is big enough for both of us."

Invitingly she turned back her covers and moved over a little on the seat. I sat down beside her, and she helped me tuck the blanket in on my side.

Man, I thought, you are certainly making progress! Here you are scarcely out of the station yard and already you're playing footsy with the manager of probably the most profitable enterprise in the whole district.

Intern experience had taught me that whores regard a physician as a member of a third sex. They neither expect nor desire him to qualify as an ardent male. Besides, I thought, didn't old Solomon say, "If two lie together, then they have heat"? I knew I craved heat. If snuggling down beside a soiled dove would damn me, at least I'd be damned in comfort.

My new friend followed the customs of hospitality of the time in Utah, which was a dry state, and brought forth a bottle of home brew, known locally as Panther Milk. She offered me the first drink.

"No, thanks," I said. I had had previous experience with this nectar.

Thereupon she turned to her recruits. "Girls," she said, "this doc has an ulcer of the stomach, and I am glad of it."

"What makes you say that?" I asked her. I had no ulcer. Not being copper-lined, I simply did not want to expose my stomach walls to such combustible brews.

"Listen," she said, "in our line of work we expect to get crowned from time to time by some beer-bottle confetti. When we get hurt we want repairs made by a man who can see only one head while he's working on it."

She added that the two previous doctors had been lushes, too drunk all the time they remained in camp to tie up a sore toe.

"The drunker other men get," she concluded, "the easier it is to separate them from their lettuce. Doctors we prefer sober when we need them. And that might be any time."

"How did you guess I'm a doctor?" I asked.

"Because you're dressed so funny."

I blinked at her.

"Call me Mamie," she said.

I never did learn her last name.

"Anyone who'd ever been on the desert," she went on, "would expect it to be a sea of mud during the winter. You better trade those fancy boots for some four-buckle over-shoes soon as you can find a sucker. There ain't ten feet of sidewalk in the whole region except the depot platform. No rattlesnake is fool enough to try to crawl around in the muck, so you don't need to worry about your ankles."

I had plenty of other questions for Mamie. It occurred to me that I had tapped the voice of experience, and I never had a chance to cork it up short of our destination, which we reached some five hours later.

First of all I wanted to know why all those fugitives from skid row were going to Wendover.

The hiring halls and the police of Salt Lake City and Sacramento, California, Mamie told me, had an arrangement whereby the cops dragged in the skid row bums. Then the labor contractors gave each wino a one-way ticket to Wendover, and the police got him on the train and out of town.

"Just what the police get out of it," she said, "is none of our business."

Some of the men would rather work than starve. They were under no contract to work, however. The construction company would feed a man for one day. Thereafter he could work or he could catch a freight train out, as suited his fancy.

"That's the way railroads get built," Mamie said.

My first duty, it appeared, would be to treat the men for their D.T.'s and see that the cook filled them up so that their wine-soaked bodies would have something to work on.

I asked her what a soogan is.

It turned out to be a cotton comforter covered with some slick material that was harder for lice to cling to than the rough surface of a blanket. The greasier his soogan looked, the more likely a man was to be picked by a construction boss. A greasy soogan denoted work camp experience.

Right then one of the girls named Pearlie butted into Mamie's discourse.

Pearlie insisted on telling me the story of her life. She was in the business, she said, to help her younger brother through medical school.

As an intern I had heard the same sad tale many times before. If it was true, half the doctors in practice got there only as the result of a sister's shame.

Mamie too got autobiographical. She had run houses in

Rhyolite and Goldfield in Nevada, and had seen many a mining camp grow, flourish, wither and die. She had grub-staked miners and fallen in love with card sharps. She had got paper-rich on mining stocks and like most other damned fools had held off so long in disposing of them that she saw her life of luxury go up in smoke. She was firmly convinced that money made in mining camps came from the suckers and not from the ground.

Sensing that here was a goldmine of the kind of information I most lacked and needed, I asked her how doctors operated in such places.

First she enlightened me on the best method for bringing back to consciousness a victim of chloral hydrate, commonly known as knock-out drops.

"You just walk him around," she said, "and slap his face."

I asked her about the types of injuries most common there. I imagined they would be gunshot or pistol wounds.

Mamie hooted at this notion. Bartenders in the saloons and bouncers in the sporting houses were always on the watch for trigger-happy customers. Any character they suspected of being so disposed, or becoming so, awoke the next morning with a cracked head and his guns hammered out of shape and usefulness. Swinging beer bottles and billiard cues was all in good fun and perfectly decorous, but gun play was beyond the conventions of polite society. In Mamie's opinion the only people who ever showed any disposition to resort to firearms were city slickers who thought such behavior would add to their social standing in local society.

"It ain't likely," she said, "you'll ever see a gunshot wound, unless it's some drunken cowboy trying to clean a loaded rifle. In that case, don't bother. They're better off dead anyhow."

On and on through the night Mamie talked. She was a good raconteur, and in spite of my previous sleepless night

I preferred to listen to her stories of mining camp life than to doze off. I could sleep some other time, but I might not get again such pictures from anyone who had both seen and taken an active part in this phase of history. Besides, she was a big, fat, good-natured animal and she gave off heat like a hot pad. To use my Missouri vernacular, I cuddled up next to her like a sick kitten to a hot brick.

When we arrived at Wendover about five A.M., Mamie kindly invited me to come along with her and the girls and spend the night at her place. I refused regretfully. They departed for the Blue Goose, as Mamie's establishment was called, in a covered wagon known locally as a "white top."

The men all headed for the little waiting room of the depot. I followed them.

They flopped down around the stove. Pretty soon I was reminded of a story I had heard about three candidates being initiated into a fraternal order. Each was shut into a small closet with a male goat and required to remain there for three minutes to qualify for lodge honors. The first two stood it for two minutes each, then had to burst out and give up. The third man had a severe case of halitosis, and after two minutes out came the goat.

In the variation of this joke played out in that waiting room, I was the goat. The railroad car had been so drafty that after my first whiff I had not noticed the odor. Perhaps Mamie's rank perfume had helped too. But in the hot little box of a waiting room the air got frowsty in a hurry.

As I stepped out on the station platform I saw the little ark which had carried us all to Wendover sailing off to Salt Lake City on the tail of a freight train—back for another load of human bodies soaked in alcohol. The Western Pacific Railway had my sympathy. Cattle cars with straw in them would have been about right for the Wendover business.

Day was breaking, so I walked around a bit to look the location over.

The town of Wendover lay just behind the station. It consisted of about fifty little shacks made out of old railroad ties and roofed with discarded gasoline cans that had been beaten out flat. There was not a tree or a bush or a blade of grass in sight. The ground was covered with empty tin cans, broken beer bottles, rusty bedsteads and bedsprings, abandoned automobile bodies and defunct cookstoves.

Further on I discovered a little store made out of concrete blocks, and a hotel which had once been painted. It was known as The Conley House.

Fifty yards behind this building rose high bluffs. Not even a weed softened their barren ugliness.

To the east and the south the landscape seemed absolutely flat. It was as white as though it lay under a blanket of fresh snow. This, however, was only the salt crust spread over what had once been an enormous inland sea. The wind was blowing, and I was to learn it always did sweep over this wilderness.

Off to the south I spied a herd of very sportive animals. They were skipping about, and occasionally one would leap up into the air in a gigantic jump.

Surely, I thought, the buffalo are all gone from here. If not, what would they find to eat on this salt bed?

I stopped a passing trainman and asked him what these animals were.

"Animals?" he laughed. "They're nothing but empty boxes and barrels."

The wind, he explained, whipped these up from the garbage dump of the construction camp kitchen, blew them off eight or ten miles during the night, and the next day blew them back to the railroad grade. This maneuver was repeated every day, seven days a week.

Then he called my attention to a smaller bluff halfway between us and the mountains to the west. He pointed out the peak of a huge tent that showed at the southern tip of it.

"That there," he said, "is the company cook tent. Those are mules stretched out behind it in picket lines."

"It looks like a circus outfit," I said. "Where are the elephants?"

"Stick around here long enough and you'll see them," he said. "Pink and blue ones at that."

Here was the end of my rainbow. Here was my Shangri-La.

I grabbed my bag and started down the railroad track to my destiny.

The Call of the Goose

The first structure I came to was the shack of the Superintendent of the construction camp. This was a lonely eight-by-ten-foot tar-paper hut, which I recognized as the boss man's because his name was on the door.

Like all other superintendents, he dwelt in solitary grandeur. He slept on an iron cot that had springs, he had a desk made of an old packing crate, and he had an armchair. These perquisites helped establish him and keep him quite high on the rigid social order of the construction camps that flourished in the era of the building of the West. Now they have all but disappeared from the American scene.

The Superintendent turned out to be a nice guy, but he was efficiency itself. That morning and all the time I worked with him he neither talked nor thought about anything but the job. He took me to breakfast, and afterward spared enough time from his work to acquaint me with my duties, assign me a little pick-up truck in which to make my rounds, indicate the general layout of the camp, and wish me well. All this he accomplished within a space of ten minutes.

For the next hour or so I wandered through the dirt, the mud, and the confusion of braying jackasses and quarreling dogs, to figure out for myself the map of the camp he had verbally sketched for me.

The Superintendent's shack was followed by more buildings of like dimensions, each of which was the nightly habitation of two of the lesser brass. But whereas the boss had

15

a cot, the lower echelons slept in bunk beds made of rough lumber and on straw bed ticks and such bedding as they might be able to acquire by fair means or foul. The boss may have a pillow and a white pillowcase on which to lay his head; the others have to be satisfied with an old coat wrapped around anything that comes handy, from shoes to extra underwear.

The workers themselves slept in bunks in tents that accommodated from fifteen to twenty men. The bunks were arranged in tiers of three. It was considered proper, should the man above you hang his dirty foot over the side of the bunk so that it brushed your face, to light a match and apply it in such a way that he withdrew the offending member. If incorrectly administered, this rebuke sometimes caused a fight, but due to the cramped quarters the scuffle was limited and neither party suffered much damage.

The camp cook dwelt in grandeur equal to that of the superintendent, but in a tent. This was close to his base of operation, and was distinguished by a rolled canvas kept under his bed. When the canvas was unrolled, it revealed an assortment of butcher knives of many shapes and sizes, all ground to a razor edge, plus a gallon jug of whisky. Any men who applied for a position as cook in a construction camp without this knife roll and a comfortable cargo of alcohol sloshing around his innards would have been sent about his business as an impostor.

The cook's kitchen help, known as "swampers," did all the dirty work, such as washing dishes, scouring pots and scrubbing floors. They slept in the cook-dining tent. In winter they would pull the dining tables up around the stove and use them for beds.

The other men of the camp were assigned to tents according to their qualifications and skills. The gang foreman was boss of the tent. Snobbery prevailed among them just as it does in any other gathering of Americans. The line of ascension was as marked as in a hen coop. The youngest men slept in the highest bunk or at the greatest distance from the stove. The poor bastard who didn't claim any particular skill washed dishes and got cussed by everybody.

The rock workers and blasting-powder men held themselves aloof from the common herd. In the grading gangs the teamsters barely concealed their contempt for the men who held the handles of the scraper while it was being loaded or unloaded. Though these teamsters drove the mules that pulled the scraper, they would never touch its handles, even if it never got loaded.

In the track gangs the spikers looked down on the characters who placed the railroad ties. All of them high-hatted the poor muckers, who smoothed the grade with shovels, and the kitchen swampers.

But the real aristocrats were the temperamental locomotive engineers, called "hog heads." If the sun didn't get up to see them pull on their cotton gloves and climb into their cabs, it was just the sun's hard luck.

In the dining tent, the Cabots—the foremen and hog heads—spoke to us Lowells at the table bearing the oilcloth, but we were supposed to communicate only with each other and God, except on business matters.

My place at the oilcloth-covered table was Number Six. This was supposed to designate my importance to the operation, and also make clear to me the five men to whom I was expected to say "Mister."

The common herd sat at tables made of rough lumber with sawhorse supports. When the festive board had accumulated too much gravy, it was turned over. We all sat on wooden benches, each of which was built to accommodate ten men. The tableware consisted of white enamel plates, mush bowls and cups and saucers. Tin cups were used for water, and there were tin knives, forks and spoons. The knives were useless, so we used our pocket knives when we were lucky enough to be served steak. This was not a frequent occurrence, for beef goes a lot further in stew.

The diet was adequate but monotonous. Eggs were always scrambled. Because of their uncertain age boiling them would have been foolhardy, and when they were fried their yolks didn't look so good. Treats were an orange or a banana for Sunday breakfast, or, for a green vegetable, canned peas. Dessert was always pie—dried apple, dried peach or dried apricot. The flour used for the crust was well diluted with cement. Even after forty years, just writing about it makes my stomach begin to buck around and swear. Every meal was accompanied by Arbuckle's coffee.

Arbuckle's was the first packaged coffee ever sold. It was rumored that it was made of navy beans soaked in carbolic acid with chewing tobacco added for coloring. I have heard it said that just after one of Brigham Young's wives had served him a cup of this potent brew he had his vision in which the Lord told him to class coffee along with tobacco and whisky as a sin.

For an office and storeroom I was assigned an area of five square feet in the headquarters building. This building also was made of rough lumber covered with tar paper; it was about twenty feet wide and forty long. The shelves, desks and stools had all been made on the job out of scrap lumber and discarded boxes.

I was given living quarters in the chief engineer's shack, and thus became one of the tar-paper nobility. This meant that I could sport a bag for my things. A workman's other suit of underwear and his socks were kept wrapped up in his bedroll in the daytime and under his head at night. Thus they were kept from wandering off and finding a new owner.

My engineer roommate had built bridges over or tunnels under almost every stream and mountain between Utah and the West Coast. He was a good storyteller and loved a joke, and he had a natural wit which could lighten up any dreary day. For down-and-outers he had great sympathy, and he never judged anybody. The reason was, he explained, that he could be proud of only two things: he had never pimped for a diseased whore or stolen house-building material from a blind tumblebug.

Since he could not drive a car himself, he traveled with me on my rounds along the proposed right of way, and while I was tending the sick he inspected the engineering problems. I learned to love that old man like a father.

When a shipment of men arrived at headquarters I looked them over. Those with chronic diseases I eliminated as worthless to the company, and also those who had some contagious disease that would spread infection. I had to be pretty strict because the company needed workers and this was a contract job for me. As the Superintendent aptly put it, what was good for my pocket was also good for the construction company. Any man I turned down was given a ticket back to where he had come from, anyway.

After I had passed them, new men were put into the cook's charge. He marched them down to one of the many warm lakes conveniently situated around the edge of the desert, and forced them to get into it and bathe. If they survived that shock, they were taken to the cook tent and given hot black coffee in mush bowls. Most of them had the shakes so badly from drinking that they could not handle a cup with one handle, but they could lean over and lap from the bowls without raising them from the table. Next, each man had to gulp down at least a pint of canned tomatoes. If that stayed down for an hour, he got a good breakfast of ham and eggs, oatmeal, and coffee with canned cream.

As time went on, and man in his wisdom discovered vitamins, I often wondered just how those old cooks ever happened to latch on to the idea that tomatoes contain some ingredient good for a man who has been living for weeks on alcohol exclusively. If canned tomatoes had not arrived soon after the rare and juicy buffalo steaks disappeared from menus, the desert regions of the West would still be a barrier to progress.

The situation in the camp was, as they say in the Navy, "normal, all fouled up." The mining company had made its survey for the railroad during the summer. The level salt flats had then seemed so admirably designed for running a straight line across them that the surveyors ignored the hill route just to the west. But now the November storm that drove me in from the car platform in Salt Lake City had reached the desert, bringing plenty of moisture with it.

The dirt that had been used to build up the railroad grade was half salt. Salt and water combine readily. The result is salt water, which is all right for ships but not for railroad engines.

There is no more distressing sight than watching a locomotive settle down into mud, especially salt mud, like an old hen on a setting of eggs. The men grew frantic, jacking up the engine and trying to rescue the rails and ties, which seemed halfway down to China. When things go wrong, as they were going then, a lot more workers get hurt than when progress is easy. I had a deluge of injuries to care for, though no very serious ones.

I had to be close to the scene of action at such distressing times. All of us got covered with the foul-smelling salt mud. I quickly discarded my fancy boots and pants and donned overalls like everyone else in the camp. If we carelessly dropped our pants on the floor at night, all the wrinkles dried stiff, reinforced with salt. The skin on our legs would give out before the salt was softened by fresh mud and water. As many people who have bathed in Salt Lake have found out, skinned or chapped areas on the legs, plus strong salt water, are not conducive to tranquility.

So we learned to hang up our pants at night. In the

morning they would be crusted with a half inch of dried salt, and when we put them on they felt like a couple of stove pipes.

Riding on a work train over, that uncertain roadbed was like riding in a small boat in a heavy sea. The only difference was that our sea had a shallow bottom of sorts. Somehow, though, we wallowed and swore our way through, and got the rails laid across the salt flats before Christmas.

The art of building a railroad in those days, before machines became cheaper than men, is now a lost one. First came the survey party, whose business it was to find the easiest grade between two points. About every hundred feet they would drive little pine stakes with queer figures on them which only the foreman could read. These designated the center of the proposed track and the height of the fill required before the ties could be laid.

Then, after cross-sectioning and more stakes, men and mules came along and plowed up the ground on each side of the roadbed-to-be. This was the borrow pit. After the ground was loosened, a second gang came with mule-drawn scrapers and shoved the loose dirt into piles roughly the shape and height of the proposed roadbed.

The muckers smoothed these piles down by hand. They were followed by a work train made up of a little engine pushing three flat cars. The first two of these were loaded with ties. Men working in teams carried the ties ahead and laid them the proper distance apart on the new grade. When they were about fifty feet beyond the end of the track, some other men brought a rail from the third car and laid it along the ties.

This last group carried the rail in big pairs of ice tongs with long handles. A man on each side of the rail held one handle, and the bite of the tongs fastened over the flange of the rail. This was a safety measure. If one man slipped and fell, the rail would drop between him and his partner without injuring either. There were about ten men on each side of a rail, and ten tongs to a rail; if the rails were carried otherwise, a spill could damage several men.

After the rail carriers came the spikers with spikes and angle irons to fasten the new rail to the one behind it and to the ties. The boss man carried a track gauge that determined the new rail's distance from its parallel fellow, and some men with bars held it steady until others could spike it into permanent position.

The joints of these thirty-foot rails were staggered every fifteen feet. There had to be a little crack between the ends of the rails at each joint to allow for expansion in hot weather; otherwise the sun could twist those steel rails until they looked like pretzels. The car wheels clicking over the little joints would sing a lullaby to oldtime passengers and soothe their nerves at night better than Miltown ever will.

When there was twenty feet of new track ahead, the work engine pushed ahead that much, and the whole process began again. Sometimes we made a mile a day—in winter the work day was from eight to five and the average wage was two dollars a day—but it took a lot of sweat, snuff and chewing tobacco to get us there. When we quit at night, the new track looked as though a child had drawn it on the living room wall. But the ballasting gangs were always a few miles back of us, and when they got the rocks and cinders pounded tight beneath and between the ties, you had a railroad.

Out there on the workings a man quickly showed what social stratum of the camp he belonged in. Back in the bunk house many a self-styled spiker would brag about his abilities, then miss the spike with his hammer when he was on the job. Fifteen minutes after he had picked up the hammer he would be promoted back to a muck stick.

There was always a team of test mules which a man who claimed he was a skinner was given to drive. The mules would work all right until the scraper was loaded, but then they would not pull an ounce unless the skinner talked to them through the lines from his hands to their bits, or from his mouth into their ears, in a language they could understand. Every man drives differently as well as rides differently. A horse or a mule knows when a man picks up the lines whether he is an experienced driver or rider. Like cows and dogs they are quick to size up the human family and react accordingly. A real mule skinner knows when to cuss loudly or softly in order to get the best performance from his team.

I was raised in the mule state of Missouri, and I supposed I had inherited the knack of driving mules. One morning just for fun I tried it, but the only way I could get the mules to move that load was to walk in front of them with a plug of battle-axe tobacco sticking out of my hip pocket. They loved eating tobacco, and they would have followed old Mamie from the Blue Goose if she had showed them some.

Somewhere during that long conversation with Mamie on the train from Salt Lake City to Wendover I had confessed to her that the real reason I was going into this work was that I was deeply in debt. Her motherly instincts were apparently aroused by this information, for she made it a point to see that I was called in when trouble occurred. Previously the bartenders had been in the habit of repairing the damage. Mamie also saw to it that my fees were promptly collected.

I did not mind the sly digs of the office force about my growing practice across the Nevada line until Mamie's workers began to get into the act in a big way. It would seem that all women in times of stress and gloom fancy themselves blessed with the gifts of the divine Sarah Bernhardt. When Mamie's girls felt abused and alone they would swallow a bit of chloral hydrate with pretended suicidal intent, and then yell bloody murder for the doctor for fear that they might have been successful.

After I had lost a few nights' sleep I grew tired of pumping stomachs. I began looking around for some place where I could make myself less available for these histrionics.

I was getting bored with the payroll aristocracy of the base camp, and I had already discovered that the best cook in the camps was at Salt Springs, a black point jutting out into the white salt about twenty miles to the south of Wendover. So I moved my headquarters to this track-laying camp in the desert.

This was a work-train camp; that is, kitchen, dining room and dwelling space were all housed in converted box cars that could be moved without difficulty to a spur track near the rail head. Everyone slept in bunks arranged somewhat like the berths in old-fashioned sleeping cars, except that they were three high, instead of two, and they were not converted into seats in the daytime. Each car had a big stove in the middle, with a space around it large enough to accommodate five or six homemade stools. At night this space functioned as a lounge for the residents.

I welcomed the opportunity for such close contacts with the labor force because I was full of curiosity about their history and their points of view. Besides, I felt a bond of sympathy with them.

It wasn't too long since I had been working for wages myself and hating my so-called superiors. I was at the age when most men are worried about mankind in general and feel themselves dedicated to correcting all the ills of the human race. Here was a good place for me to hear expounded the wild ideologies to which youth is most susceptible.

I was on my way to becoming a firm believer in some of these and so expressed myself. Then one of the most vocal advocates of the new order took me outside one evening and read me a quiet lecture.

"Son," he said, "don't get too interested in all this classless society and equal division of wealth stuff. It is wonderful to dream about and preach, but any man who knows human nature also knows it won't work. Without envy man would run down like a watch with a broken mainspring. Take envy away and what is left to work for? Call it ambition if you wish, but it's *envy*.

"If everybody here had an equal amount of money and knew the state would feed him, this railroad would never get built.

"Besides, history tells us that whenever any group, be it political, industrial or religious, did not have a strong opposition to curb it, despotism quickly developed. For amusement the despots would kill off all the non-conformists. History will repeat itself one of these days. Talk it if you want to, but thank God every night that you live in a time when you can bitch about anything without fear of punishment."

My mentor did not look like the pictures of the prophets in the Bible. His stubby gray whiskers were stained with tobacco juice, his eyes were red and bleary from alcohol, and his body was wasted from dissipation. But the last twenty years have proved he ranked up there with Jeremiah.

Oh well, we all have to grow up sometime, and it was about time for me to start. I began thinking about some advice an old and wise physician had given me when I went to tell him goodbye before leaving Missouri for the West.

"This profession of which you are now a member," he explained, "is made up of art and science. There isn't very much science to it, so you should try to perfect yourself in the art. The art of medicine consists of a few simple rules: have an honest interest in your patient's welfare, know his family and his working environment, have sympathy with his ambitions and compassion on his failures, and let him know that your thoughts are on his recovery first and your fee second."

Sometimes I think that science has crowded art too far out of the picture in these latter days.

Here was a fertile field in which to cultivate some of that art, which even we medical students of fifty years ago heard little about in school, and I began to do so.

It began to pay dividends right away. The cook invited me to dine with him, and we had T-bone steaks while the menu offered only beans. The men made me more welcome at their nightly gatherings, and called me Doc.

Many of the men were old hands at construction jobs, and could speak with the authority of experience of such far-away places as Prince Rupert Island and Santiago, Chile, and the women who dwelt there as well as the construction jobs and the scenery. While sitting around the bunk car stoves at night I was surprised to find that many of them were more than well-educated. Some had even held responsible positions in society, but had fallen because of the mistaken belief that if they got drunk their troubles would disappear for a while at least.

Most of them, however, were the castoffs of society. A more varied collection of oddballs would have been hard to get together. Their moral sense toward society was almost completely lacking; they lived from one debauch to the next and suffered no more pangs of conscience than an alley cat. They would fight among themselves, but they banded together at the first sign of attack by social institutions on one of their number or their friends.

Once word came down from Wendover that the County Sheriff had arrived there, had inquired about the camp doctor, and had later set off toward Salt Springs to find me. Almost before I heard about it over the telephone, men were slipping into my quarters offering me getaway money and advice as to spots to which I could disappear for a while and where no questions would be asked if I but mentioned who had sent me. Because I elected to await the coming of this their natural enemy, I was considered a fool. The men's credo was hide and find out his intentions from ambush.

These kind of "boomers" have pretty well faded from the scene, their places taken by unromantic machines. But they did the world's dirty work when dirty work had to be done, and they conformed to no pattern of behavior or appearance except as their whims dictated. Their attitude was that it was their money and their life, and they would spend either or both as they pleased.

Many things about them a member of a more ordered society was compelled to abhor, but they had one trait in common that was a cut above the average among men in more secure stations of life—though organized society was their common enemy, all animal life below the human they treated in a kind and gentle manner.

I never saw a work animal abused or struck unnecessarily with the whip without the man responsible being justly dealt with by his fellows. Most dogs in western Utah and eastern Nevada ran away from home and attached themselves to these derelicts with a fidelity beyond understanding. Even the little snow birds, or juncos, lost all fear and would sit on outstretched hands to pick cracked grain from the palm.

The camp was close to the warm sloughs, and so ducks were everywhere about it. No one would bother to clean and pick a duck, as these birds soon found out. They discovered a free lunch counter on the mules' picket line and at the back door of the cook car. The latter, the dogs felt, was their special territory and so they would chase the ducks, who would then soar off and sail around our heads, quacking with a roar like a jet plane. In general the desert is deathly silent, but it was not around that camp.

One morning while we were eating breakfast we heard a new note in this barnyard symphony. It was like a French horn in full throttle. Every fork and spoon dropped to the table, and we rushed to the door. Outside was an enormous Canada goose using his one good wing to fight off a couple of dogs which he was cursing roundly in goose language.

The appearance of so many of his natural enemies confused the honker, and he made a break for the safety of the water. This move gave the dogs their chance to attack his rear and grab a few mouthfuls of feathers from that tender region. But a kitchen swamper rushed out and kicked the dogs away, allowing the visitor to make a more or less dignified retreat into the swamp.

Geese were a rarity in Deep Creek Country, for there were no wheat fields within a hundred miles for them to glean, as they love to do in the winter time. The drooping and useless wing explained the presence of this grand specimen.

The men saw in him a kindred spirit in trouble, and reacted as if he were a lodge brother. One man was detailed to guard the area around the swamp, and another was sent for grain to scatter on the bank. The dogs, unaccustomed to such cursing and kicking, retired to the bluff behind the camp to await their masters' return to sanity, and we returned to breakfast.

As anyone knows who has ever hunted geese, the expression "crazy as a goose" is a compliment. Those snake-like heads are crammed full of intelligence and an ability to outthink the hunter most of the time. This one decided that it was better to risk being eaten than to starve to death. By nightfall he was strutting around the camp, and within a couple of days he would allow us to feed him from our hands.

The boys worried a lot about his useless wing. They caught him and brought him into my office area and insisted that I put splints on it. To please them, I examined the wing and found that the bone had been broken by a rifle bullet. I bound it to his side with bandages and adhesive tape, but as I expected he would do, within fifteen minutes he had torn the dressings off. Nature did a better job than I could do. Within a week he was able to fold the wing close to his body, and in a month he could use it to fly up to the top of the cars.

He did not need the wing in camp, however, for he learned merely to come to the car steps and honk. There was always someone handy to lift him up. He would walk along behind us as we sat at the long tables; then suddenly that black head would shoot in under a man's arm and scoop up a piece of pie or some other choice morsel so quickly that one could hardly see the action. The men became experts in eating with their elbows close to their bodies instead of sprawling all over the table as had been customary.

At night the goose showed no inclination to return to the water to roost, and so, of course, he was taken into the bunk car, where he would sit in front of the stove preening his feathers or sleeping while the men talked. That enormous gander would squat in the light of the stove door, which was kept open so that the men could spit into it, while a dozen men sat around on nail kegs or the edges of the bunks in tobacco smoke so thick that the smoky old lantern hanging from the ceiling shed a light as soft as that seen through a thin fog.

When the bottle went round the goose was given a piece of bread soaked in whisky, but he did not carry his likker very well. He stumbled around and honked and honked for no apparent reason, and so it was decided that the goose at least should be a total abstainer.

The old-timers complained about his presence, claiming that they could not romance their tales of far-off places with that goose sitting there listening. Whenever they told a big one, they said, that bird would open one eye and honk in derision. They argued that he had been over the same ground and knew when their accuracy left something to be desired. I tried to persuade them that the goose honked when the other men laughed, but I could not convince them.

They speculated a good deal about his masculine attributes. No one was certain that he was a male, but in that company he just had to be. Some kind souls were all for sending to the city for a tame lady goose to keep him company, but this proposal was voted down. Even a female goose would be in danger of improper advances from some of those characters. Besides females always curdle the milk of human kindness and fellowship when they intrude into a purely masculine world.

If the goose was lonesome he did not let it interfere with his routine. As his wing recovered he showed himself a match for any dog at the camp. He appointed himself camp policeman and watchman. If a stranger approached, he lit into him with his head down and his wings cocked for action and hissed like a locomotive blowing off steam. One day Mr. Christensen, the General Manager, came out. The bird took up his station at the car steps and would not let Christensen pass until the boys pulled him away. After that the men did love him—a wild free soul that hated authority in any form.

In February the camp moved to within a mile of Errickson's Ranch. The only water there in which the goose could take the daily swim he loved was the ranch pond. So when the work train set out in the morning he rode on the flat cars with the men until they came to the pond. Here the train stopped and left the goose and his bodyguard for the day. The guard was considered necessary to protect the goose from the occasional hunters who came by. The straw bosses, of course, knew about this arrangement, but if the construction company officers had known they were paying wages to a goose-sitter, almost anything might have happened.

About two P.M. the pair would start walking home down the newly laid track. A goose is a poor walker and a slow ground-gainer anywhere, and on the railroad ties this one made a pathetically awkward sight. But he objected to being carried, and so the two seldom got home much before the shift train.

One Sunday morning during breakfast the goose became very excited, honking and beating his wings against the door. When it was opened, he tumbled to the ground and honked and honked with all his considerable lung power. For a minute or two no one could find a reason for this behavior. Then we too heard a far-off honking, and pretty soon we spotted a V of geese flying very high to the east of us.

Our boy redoubled his vocal efforts. The response must have been favorable, because with a mighty beating of wings and what seemed to be hoots of joy he took off.

We watched him until he had joined his kind and was lost with them from view. Then we returned to a breakfast that had somehow lost its flavor and zest.

We had heard that geese mate for life. Although none of the men ever acknowledged any marital ties, they all hoped that his wife was in that flock he had joined. If she were not, however, after what he had learned from association with our mob, he should have been able to steal some other gander's giddy mate without too much trouble. And with the practice he had gained licking dogs, he should have been able to overthrow the leader of the flock and guide his followers to nesting grounds in full command of the situation.

After he was gone, the men joked about him in a rather

loud and strained fashion. Then somehow the evening gatherings grew more subdued and subject to long silences. We could read one another's thoughts. Every man, while wishing the goose health, happiness and success in love, was also consumed with envy at his inborn wildness and freedom.

Poor earthbound creatures, by nature unfitted to face life's problems without the heartening effects of whisky, still they envied one who could resume his place so easily in the society of his fellows. They have all been dead these many years, and I am sure the great Judge took into consideration their poor equipment for life when He passed upon their misspent years. Who knows, perhaps like the thief of Cavalry they now have wings, and can follow the flight of the wild goose.

Christmas with Mamie

Some time after the middle of December the mania which affects all Christian nations about that time of year began to manifest itself, however improbably, in Salt Springs.

The cook sent the swampers out into the surrounding hills for greenery, and they decorated the dining car with boughs of desert juniper—a dirty, grayish-green little tree that smells worse than it looks. They found one bunch of desert mistletoe, which is pink-stemmed and sports pink berries, and hung it over the entrance—not that they expected anybody to get kissed under it, but as one swamper remarked, "It looks fitting and you never can tell what will turn up on the desert." And one homesick artist dug out a can of red paint and touched up some of the gray berries on the juniper so that they more nearly resembled the traditional holly branches.

Everyone grew progressively more restless. Conversation changed around the evening fires too. The advantages of the Latin girls from south of the border over their colder sisters of northern latitudes was no longer the central point of argument. Instead the men's talk and memories turned to former Christmas seasons and the way in which they had been celebrated. Some of the tales were ribald and many of them dealt with monumental drunks, but everybody listened when some poor guy told about the simple observances of his childhood.

33

Because the weather had dried up a bit and we were making good progress with the ballasting and track laying, all of us knew that our Christmas vacation would be a short one. We were way behind schedule and the company intended to lay track as long as the sun shone. There was some grumbling to the effect that anybody should know such an important occasion ought to be celebrated by a week's drunk at least. All we were to have was one day on the condition that we make it up by working the next Sunday. We cheerfully agreed to do this, and everyone made plans for his holiday. We would close up camp Christmas Eve and all go to Wendover and hope that hellhole would look a little less like what it was for that one day at least.

As could have been expected, December twenty-fourth was ushered in by the worst snow storm of the winter and heartfelt curses by everybody. No doubt kids would have enjoyed it, but we knew of no kids in Deep Creek Country. To us adult orphans a white Christmas meant only more washouts, more delays, and more mud.

We started early for Wendover. Our engineer planned to catch a fast freight for Salt Lake City on arrival at Wendover, and so he took chances with the steam throttle, with the result that we all landed in the mud about ten miles from our destination. That meant piling out into the storm in our clean clothes, grabbing shovels, jacks and re-railers and digging like crazy until we had those pony trucks back on the rails. It was after midnight when we got her back on the track. By that time every man looked as if he were wearing over his entire body a plaster cast composed of mud and salt, stiff and smelly.

The town had gone to bed. The only visible sign of Christmas cheer was a red lantern hanging over the door of the Blue Goose which was intended to advertise the establishment rather than to honor the season. I crawled into my old bunk in the chief engineer's hut without even looking at my mail and packages I had ordered held there, and shivered and shook until four A.M. before I could get to sleep. I had not built a fire for fear of disturbing my dear old roommate's sleep, but I was mighty happy when he disturbed mine about five o'clock by starting one himself.

I was not so happy, though, a half hour later when he shook me and asked me to get up because he was ill and needed me. The only piece of clothing I had discarded was my coveralls, so I was up with my stethoscope in one hand and a thermometer in the other almost before he quit shaking me. These he motioned away, saying his sickness could not be diagnosed or cured by ordinary medical procedures.

"Just sit down," he ordered, "and listen to the case history, and then we will consider therapeutics."

It was the same old story I had heard in the bunk cars— a man of good family, fine training and brilliant mind with a bright future ahead of him. Hard work and worry had led him to take a drink in an effort to ease his tensions. But he was just the type of man who should never touch the stuff, for like so many geniuses he had an unstable nervous system. Once he began to drink he went the whole hog and stayed drunk for a week at a time. Between spells of craving, however, he never touched the stuff.

Five years earlier he had been next to the top in the engineering division of a great transcontinental railroad. This present dinky job was the last stop before skid row welcomed him. They had taken him back time and again, and even now had told him that if he stayed on the job until this road was built they would give him another chance.

Christmas and the memories of other, different Christmases had been more than he could stand. His whole body was crying for the oblivion of a drunken stupor. He had even stuffed his pants into the fire in the hope that having to run half a mile in his shirttail to get a drink might overcome his impulses. Now he was about crazy.

Damn old Osler anyhow! I never saw a case to which his big *Principles and Practice of Medicine* applied. All of mine were oddballs, and I had to think up treatments out of my own head.

I knew this old man was fond of a silly card game called pinochle in which you meld and unmeld and can play all day without wearing out any brain cells. I suggested we play a few hands while we thought about what to do with him.

He won the first game, but when I saw him licking his lips and looking at the door I took advantage of his inattention and beat the socks off him for the next hour or so. By that time he was thinking about cards, and when I mentioned breakfast he insisted that we have it brought to the cabin. He was sure I could not hold him if he got within a hundred yards of the Nevada line. So we ate sandwiches for breakfast and for lunch too, and from six A.M. until seven P.M. we played that fool game as though we had a hundred-dollar pot. Then he decided he was over his craving and that we should go up to the Western Pacific lunch room and have turkey. Soon after this supper he retired.

I sneaked over to the cook tent to get a taste of the Christmas cheer—the office force celebration, to which I had contributed, was to have consisted of a couple of washtubs of Tom-and-Jerries. The place was deserted, and there were only a few streaks of egg white left on the sides of the washtubs. What a Christmas! But at least I had my mail and packages, so I returned to the cabin and read until ten, when I too went to bed.

Before I had time to warm up the bed, the watchman came and said that Pearlie, one of the soiled doves at the Blue Goose, had drunk a whole bottle of knockout drops, and that if I did not hurry she would probably get her wish and be buried in white within a day or so.

Once again I started out to save a life which by most standards was not worth saving. I had left my stomach pump at Salt Springs, but I gave her a dose of apomorphine, which is a powerful emetic. Presently Pearlie was wishing she really could die, but soon up came the chloral hydrate along with everything else she had eaten or drunk in the last day, which was considerable.

Mamie was acting as doctor's assistant and advising the other girls how to handle the emesis basin (or bucket). When things began to quiet down she looked at me closely and said, "Doc, you look plum beat. Sit down a minute and I'll fix you something to pick you up."

It was then five A.M., and the train left at seven. There was no point in going back to bed, so I settled down in the parlor without putting a nickel in the player piano and waited for the drink which was supposed to put new life into my sleep-starved body.

Mamie fixed up some weird combinations of raw eggs, milk and pepper sauce which tasted like the contents of a fire extinguisher that carries its fire along with it. In fact, she made two of them and sat down with a groan into a chair beside me, remarking that we both needed something to warm our blood.

I was too tired to do much thinking or talking, so I asked her a question which had mildly interested me since I had come to the region.

"Why is it," I said, "that all the books one reads about mining camps and construction projects are full of the glamorous dance hall girls at the Golden Nugget Saloon, but all you have under this roof are a bunch of burned-out old cows?"

I did not expect her to get mad because in watching doctors and their female patients in the hospitals I had noticed that women take no offense when physicians talk bluntly to them. In fact, most women seem to appreciate talk from doctors which coming from other men would make them furious. I was not mistaken. Mamie kicked off her shoes, gave her girdle a hitch to the right, took a long drink, heaved forth a mighty belch and settled down to a monologue.

"Doc," she began, "I hate to do it, but I guess I was appointed to educate you about women and knock a lot of fool romantic notions out of your head.

"You being a grown man and a doctor, we will assume that you understand the differences in our physical make-up. But from the neck up all you look at is the face. You do not realize that we have a brain behind it which works altogether differently than your own. To put it on the line, let's say that men are adults with little boy's brains, and that women are all their mothers, not interested in playing war games and building silly little railroads. We feel a satisfactory superiority over you because we can produce life. Of course, you help a little, but not even George Washington could have a baby. Consequently we are not driven by the urges which prompt you males to be always creating something new to boost your egos, but direct our efforts toward getting the easy pleasures out of life as we go along.

"The greatest luxury you ever thought up for our pleasure was warm bathrooms. You invented them, but you know nothing about using them. You go there to shave and tend the calls of nature, but the south side of a rock is adequate for one and you all hate to shave and would never do it if we did not force you into it. Therefore you look upon the bathroom as a necessary nuisance, but bathrooms are the reason this place is not populated with young and attractive women instead of what you call burned-out cows.

"These cows are here because they cannot compete with the girls in our business in the city. Most of them are at the last station with nothing to look forward to but the knockout drops. Pearlie knows this, and you and I probably did her a disservice by bringing her out of it. Now in town a girl can spend half a day in the bathroom, redoing her hair, soaking in a tub full of warm perfumed water, painting her face, making new eyebrows, washing out stockings, and lord knows what else. If her companion for the night needs it she can even coax him into the tub before going to bed.

"Just suppose I had to visit the little place out back right now. First I'd have to light a lantern, then put on overshoes and a big coat and face the storm while I walked fifty yards from the back door to my destination. When I get there what do I find? A shack made of railroad ties and old Coca-Cola signs that have been shot up so badly they're no longer any use on the highway. I set down the lantern and take off the coat, and then there is nothing between my hide and the North Pole but a piece of tin full of .38 caliber bullet holes with the wind blowing through them from the north at fifty miles an hour.

"I made a piece of money on this hunch one time. I was running a house in Goldfield and doing a good business until some nut decided to build a big modern brick hotel there. When I saw all those bathtubs going in I got scared and sold out my business and invested the money in a little cottage in Pasadena, California, for my old age. After that hotel opened its doors the girls came from as far away as Sacramento to cash in on the harvest on weekends, and the dame who bought me out went broke in a year.

"No sir, business is not all sunshine for us hookers, and bathrooms are the biggest cloud in the sky. Let a female see one bathroom and she is never happy until she has one of her own, whether she is the mayor's wife or the poorest hooker on skid row."

I broke in, as she seemed to be running down. "Your argument doesn't hold water. Look at the wives of these mining engineers who are moving up to Gold Hill where they don't even have any water to bathe in, to say nothing of steam-heated bathrooms."

"It don't mean a thing, Doc," Mamie said. "Those dames

are just camping out where they can watch their men and keep them from getting so hard up these cattle will look good to them. Each and every one will yank hubby out of there by the ears as soon as she sees that he isn't going to make a pile of money to build her a marble bathroom. Yes, I've heard of Mrs. Gerster who has been there for forty years with her man. Well, there are some women in the world capable of loving a man more than a bathroom, but they are damned scarce.

"If you are going to live in the West, don't ever marry an Eastern woman. And if you expect to stay all your life in Gold Hill you had better get yourself a Gosiute squaw who has never seen a bathroom. Eastern women cannot stand the casual way of living we practice out here, and any loving bride will bean you with a hatchet if you try to keep her here too long."

It was not yet time for the train to leave so I probed a little deeper.

"But Mamie, you haven't told me about that Pasadena cottage."

She took another swallow of the restorer, burped again and continued: "Everybody has to have a goal. Mine is to leave the desert and settle down there among the flowers and orange blossoms. I am going to go respectable, join a church and learn to drink tea and be shocked proper when I hear about the carryings-on of the young folks or when anybody says damn in my presence.

"This is my last business venture. I have saved enough now to see me through. When this railroad is built I'll feel that I have done my bit for suffering masculine humanity. Once I thought of getting pious in a big way and joining a convent, but I hate those long black dresses. When the Utah Construction Company pulls out of here, Mamie leaves the next day and will never be heard of again. I'll be Mrs. Mary Johnson, the widow of a big mining man, when I get on that train and shake the salt off my feet."

One last dig and I had to go.

"But Mamie, you have lived on the desert for forty years or so. You can't get it out of your blood that easy. I'll bet you five dollars you'll tire of orange blossoms and begin pining for sagebrush in six months, and if I lose just send me a card and I'll remit without comment."

The engine whistled and I started to the door, but she called after me.

"It's a deal, and you might as well pay me now as later."

That was the last I ever saw of Mamie, but riding back in the caboose to Salt Springs, I brooded a good deal over what she had said. I had no idea how long I would be out there, and Mamie's theory that only a Gosiute squaw would be willing to settle down with me did not appeal at all. Somehow, if you're nice to the demi-monde, you always wind up feeling embarrassed.

It reminded me of a night some years before when I was a senior in medical school and on duty in the hospital accident ward. A couple of girls from the red light district were brought in, much the worse for a beating they had received in a riot at their place of business.

Another student and I fixed them up before the Senior House Officer arrived. We were quite proud of our jobs of sewing scalps and making facial repairs. So proud, in fact, that we invited several other chaps in to see our handiwork. This gesture made the girls think they were important, and they felt very kindly toward us.

After they left the hospital they sent us a case of beer in appreciation. This alone was embarrassment enough, for the school was a strict Methodist institution. It is difficult to keep hidden a large wooden box containing twenty-four quart bottles of beer while its contents are being disposed of.

Nevertheless, with the help of some noble souls we managed to get by.

One evening a short time later we were walking on the local petticoat lane with a couple of very proper young ladies. Along came a bright red dogcart with patent leather trim, drawn by ponies hitched tandem and sporting flowers on their head harness. Its two passengers were all dolled up in silks and bows of vivid and startling hues. Their make-up, which might attract no attention today, looked like a house afire then; and each was holding on her lap a tiny dog that was almost hidden by the large red bow on its collar.

We recognized our former patients. Quickly we sneaked around on the inner side of our dates and pretended to be fascinated by the window display we were passing.

But the two sunflowers had spotted us. They stopped the ponies and yelled: "Hi there, Joe and Harry! Why don't you come on down and see us?"

Our dates gave us looks that would kill squirrels at fifty yards, and ducked into the store, leaving us at the mercy of the amused shoppers. Being cowards and slaves of convention then, we dashed around the corner and lost ourselves as quickly as possible.

Now, slumped down in a corner of the caboose, I toted up the gain and loss column of my holiday: two nights with only two hours' sleep; a Christmas dinner of seagull or raven masquerading as Western Pacific Railway turkey; keeping an old man's foot from slipping off the come-back ladder; saving a life that didn't want to be saved; getting a disillusioning lecture.

As time went on, however, I was to regard that lecture as a valuable contribution to my knowledge of the psychology of women, a queer sex upon whom much of my future success as a physician was to depend. I frequently thought of Mamie.

Five years after that Christmas the Deep Creek railroad

had flourished and died. Gold Hill was again a ghost camp. I had been away at war for two years and was an old married doctor in Tooele, Utah. One morning a drug salesman called upon me. After the usual business was over he hesitated a minute, then asked me if I had ever known a lady by the name of Mrs. Johnson who once lived in California.

I said I did not. "Why?" I asked him.

"About six months ago," he replied, "I stopped for the night at a hotel in Las Vegas, Nevada. The old lady who owned the place noticed my business card and asked if I ever traveled in Utah. I told her I expected to make that state in about four months. 'When you get there,' she said, 'and should happen to call upon a Dr. Peck—I don't know where he lives—ask him if he was ever in Wendover. If he says yes, hand him this five dollar bill and tell him that he won a bet.' "

She had refused to give him further information. I did not need any more. There was talk then of a new dam being built near Vegas, and I knew Mamie believed in being in on the ground floor.

4

Ends of the Line

There was a debit I did not know about on that ledger of my so-called Christmas vacation. The first day I was back at camp I realized that my status had changed much for the worse. No longer was it "Hi, Doc, pass the beans," but, spoken to the man next to me in a voice anyone could hear, "Ask the doctor to pass the beans." And when I went into the bunk cars at night, conversation quieted down at once.

Having been a working man myself not so very long before, and having hated the company physician as a matter of principle, I could diagnose this coolness but could do nothing about it. I had prided myself that I was not like some company physicians I had known, but had consistently put the men's interests ahead of those of the company, and I felt that I was making progress in overcoming their natural distrust of one who took the king's shilling.

Because even a small amount of alcohol would give me a severe case of migraine instead of joyful stimulation, I had always passed the bottle to the next man without taking a comradely swallow. They understood and accepted that shortcoming, but could not accept the fact that I had gone off and spent my holiday on a private drunk. No one had seen me around camp during Christmas, and my haggard appearance did much to strengthen their belief. I looked a mess and felt worse because my lack of rest was intensified by a mild case of ptomaine from that railroad lunch-counter turkey. So if I was the sort of guy who would refuse a drink of fellowship but would go off on a solo drunk, I must feel too good to enjoy myself with them. I must be a nice guy for business reasons only.

I could not clear myself because there were persons around who would have loved to get something on the chief engineer. The mining company had hired a bunch of engineers just out of college to run the original survey because one of their dads was a stockholder. The contract had been made on the basis of their blueprints, but they had made some serious mistakes. Corrections cost money, and the chief engineer was not backward in billing the mining company for the extra work. The mining company people were hoping for a chance to get even and have him thrown out of there.

I had no intention of accommodating them. Besides, the doctor-patient relationship is confidential, even if this one had consisted only of a marathon of pinochle. It was either suffer it out or lie about it.

I have always regarded the truth as admirable but not necessarily obligatory. Consequently I made up a tale about a sheepherder so sick that I had to attend him for two nights and a day. The atmosphere improved immediately.

Retribution always comes quickly in my case. The recording angel does not bother to record my misdeeds, just punishes me at once. This instance was no exception. Twenty-four hours after I had been reinstated, the Wendover office telephoned that there was a very sick man at Low station, and would I go over there and see what I could do?

I had passed through Low at night, and had supposed it to be a more or less civilized community, so I dressed in my good clothes and went.

When I arrived I found it consisted of a depot and two saddle horses tied to the stockyard fence. The telegraph operators slept in the freight room and cooked their own meals on the office stove.

My patient was eight miles away in a sheep camp. A herder was waiting to guide me over the hills to him. From his story I guessed the emergency was an abdominal one of some kind.

I packed a few supplies in a saddle bag and started out on the long ride. The temperature was about fifteen above zero, the usual desert wind cut like a knife, and there was a crust on the snow that made hard going for our horses.

I had never learned to ride in such a way that my trouser legs would remain about my ankles. Every half mile I had to dismount and invite the ruffle about my knees back down to my shoe tops. Then I would grab the horse's tail and walk until my legs thawed out. If that brute had been bobtailed I never would have made it, but walking is easy when all one has to do is lift his feet while a horse furnishes the forward motion.

Before we reached the top of the last hill I had sworn a solemn vow to move someday to California, where the snowstorms are rare and mild. The desert may be beautiful, but the poets who so describe it never looked at it from the south end of a horse going north or while climbing up a ski slope on which all the rocks were covered by three inches of ice or frozen snow—just a bare white and sterile land with here and there a miserable little shad scale peeping through the crust. How the sheep managed to paw that hard frozen stuff away from the little bushes and get enough nourishment for two—for all of them were big with lamb—is still a mystery to me, who think I know a little about the nutritional requirements of the pregnant female.

It took us four hours to travel that eight miles.

The patient was in bed in the usual sheeptender's wagon. Although the air was warm, he was covered with a cold clammy perspiration. His abdomen was puffed up and as hard as a board, his temperature was below normal, and his heart was racing. It was a clear case of inflammation of the peritoneum (the lining of the abdominal cavity) and, I deduced from the history, probably a ruptured stomach ulcer to boot.

It's a funny thing about our poor long-suffering stomachs; their lining can handle the acid digestive fluids without much trouble, but let this lining get a leak in it and the juices begin at once to digest the rest of the stomach wall. When they get through that, they start in digesting all the other abdominal organs with which they come into contact. This is, I suppose, somewhat like being chewed by a tiger or being devoured by ants, except the ants are inside your belly wall and you cannot get at them. Rather an awkward situation to be in on a cold winter's day and a hundred miles from any relief.

This poor chap had tried to ease his pain by drinking Nunn's Black Oil, a carbolic acid mixture used by herdsmen and cowboys to dab on cuts and snake bites suffered by their animals. Of course, in this case it had all run out through the stomach puncture and added phenol poisoning and burning to the rest of his misery. There was no such thing then as antibiotics, and surgery held little hope. All I could do was ease the man's pain.

I decided to get him back to Low, where we could catch the evening train to Salt Lake City, where his wife lived, and a hospital. The herder took the saddles off the ponies and harnessed them to the sheeptender's wagon while I drew the live coals from the stove and threw them into the snow because sometimes these wagons turn over. I did not want to fry my patient on the outside too.

We tied an old section of harrow behind the wagon to serve as a land anchor when we were going down hillsides, and took along a stout pole to lock the rear wheels if necessary. The sheep we left in the care of a couple of intelligent dogs. All the way we prayed that the harness would not break going down hill and allow the neck yoke and wagon tongue to bury themselves in the snow and pile us all up in a heap.

It was twelve miles the way we had to travel with the wagon, and we arrived just before the train did. By midnight I had my patient in the hospital.

His anxious wife and their three little kids were waiting for us. She had chosen a surgeon and engaged a room.

The surgeon and I examined the man there. I wanted to let the poor fellow die in peace and save his family the expense of an operating room. The surgeon, however, apparently wanted to prove my diagnosis incorrect. Besides, he assured me, if we did not make a grandstand play, the family would be terribly disappointed. Survivors, I later learned, just love to tell how gallantly the doctors struggled, but "God wanted him and took him home."

So we opened up the sheeptender's belly, proved that I had been right, and probably hurried him on his way to meet the Great Shepherd. At least, the man died within a couple of hours after leaving surgery.

While we were washing up, the surgeon said: "Now, Doctor, I'll get what I can from the family. They have an insurance policy, and if we don't get part of it, the undertaker will get it all. That devil has no conscience when his customers have tears in their eyes. Whatever I get, I will divide with you seventy-five and twenty-five."

I thought he was joking. "But I have already been paid for my services," I said. "Yesterday morning his buddy killed a lynx and gave me the skin to be mounted. I don't intend to give you twenty-five per cent of that hide, not even the stubby little tail."

"I mean it," the surgeon replied. "Every young man needs help when he is starting out. I will return you twenty-five per cent of any fees I collect for surgical cases you send me. Of course, this is just between ourselves."

I could not believe my ears. From my experience with

other surgeons I had thought this practice, which I had heard damned so often, existed only in rumor. No one before or since has ever offered me anything more than a cigar. Now here I was face to face with a tempter whom I had heard stand up in medical society meetings and deplore the supposedly unethical conduct of various unnamed surgeons. I took his offer as a personal insult.

"Listen, mister," I said not too temperately, "this conversation reminds me of two old ravens I saw out by the sheep camp yesterday picking the shreds of flesh from a dead sheep's bones. If I were after that kind of money, Mamie, the boss of the Blue Goose in Wendover, would pay me more than that to pimp for her establishment."

Then he also blew his top. "Why, you . . . you . . ." he stuttered. His religion seemed to be handicaping his vocabulary. "This is the last time you'll ever bring a patient to this hospital!"

"If everyone in this hospital is like you," I said, "which I do not believe, I don't ever want to be caught in such company."

We left the preparation room by different doors. I shall never forget the horrified expression on the face of the little student nurse who was mopping up the operating room.

It was early morning of the last day of the year. I stood on the steps of that great institution dedicated to the relief of suffering humanity, and looked up at the stars shining brightly in the clear night sky. Then and there I made myself a solemn resolution, not about what I would do, but, like the chief engineer, about what I would not do: Never, so long as I might live, would I put the dollar sign in front of the Caduceus.

I kept the vow pretty well until in later years I had to deal with the WPA. The government so arranged that monstrosity that both doctors and dentists had to forsake their principles to get along with it. It would be nice if we could retain our youthful outlook and see the world only as black and white, but age dims our vision. As we mature, all sorts of gray shades enter the spectrum and we do not run so readily to the defense of purity of purpose.

Perhaps the old surgeon was just trying to help me. Even now I shudder to think what my response might have been if I had had a family to support, and no patients demanding my efforts. I was lucky when Satan showed himself to me; I was single, I was paying off my debts, and was even saving a little money.

Many times thereafter I passed that old man in the corridors of the hospital. We never spoke. I still wonder whether I should have turned him in to the medical society. Probably it was better that I did not. He died an honorable man, so the papers said. Perhaps he was, but I think he was in the wrong profession; he should have been running a loan-shark racket.

It was six A.M. when I got to a hotel in Salt Lake City. Like Mamie's fancy hookers I spent the rest of the morning in the bathtub. It felt wonderful, but it would have felt even better if I had not been doing battle with my sense of duty. It was New Year's Eve, and I certainly contemplated laying over a day in town and doing a little celebrating. If I had not indulged in such moral thoughts and actions the night before, I could have easily throttled my conscience and stayed away from my charges. But, in the end, a discouraged and disheartened young doctor caught the train back to snow, sagebrush and desolation.

Everyone seemed happy to see me when I got back. The swamper who had brought our lunch to the engineer's hut on Christmas had heard enough to know why I was not in evidence that day. He had told another swamper, and so on. Now the whole camp was laughing about the sheepherder story I had made up. They kidded me unmercifully about foretelling my own troubles, and kept asking me to predict their futures.

As a matter of fact, that same morning I was able to reveal impending disaster to one man. While I was at headquarters, a female of commanding appearance came in and asked if her husband were working on this job. She had heard a rumor in Denver that he was out here, and she had come looking for him.

The timekeeper put her off by saying he would send a note to the other timekeepers inquiring about the missing spouse. He told her to come back at five that afternoon.

I went out to bring her husband the glad tidings.

"What?" he yelled. "Is that old rhinoceros in Wendover?"

He dropped his track gauge and almost ran to the camp office, where he drew his time. Then he started to roll his pack.

"Where are you going?" I asked him.

"She is north?" he said. "Right. Then I go south."

"What'll you do, go deeper into the desert?"

He shrugged. "Herd sheep. Prospect for a mine. Sooner or later get a ride to Ely, Nevada, and get lost proper."

He caught the mail stage to Deep Creek, and that was the last we ever heard of him.

Every story of the Old West has clung to the pattern set down by Owen Wister in *The Virginian* and introduced a beautiful, kind and romantic school teacher from the sheltered atmosphere of an Eastern ladies' college, who bulldogged the wildest and most unlikely critter in the bunk house and made a gentle, housebroken husband out of him. We had such a female, but it could hardly be said that she enjoyed the same success as her fictional counterpart.

She arrived with a trunk full of riding breeches and other

equipment, just panting to fork Old Paint, ride into the corral and drop her rope over the head of the local Gary Cooper. Unfortunately Gary wasn't around. The mangy critter she did catch wasn't worth the effort and dragged her a ways in the dust before he lit out.

That was why the sheriff was looking for medical assistance.

He had arrived in Wendover in response to a telegram urging him to come and investigate a crime, only to find that the deed had been done just over the line, in Nevada. (He was a Utah officer, from Tooele, the county seat, a hundred and twenty miles away.) In Wendover he learned that the alleged culprit was in need of medical assistance. Thus, he had himself a problem. Should he return home and wire the Nevada authorities and so delay the action for two or three days? Or should he take a Utah doctor to the scene as an act of mercy?

Medical law is not so strict as the criminal code. I knew Nevada would allow a Utah-licensed doctor to give emergency care, and away we went.

We back-tracked to Wendover and then west over the Silver Zone mountains on the worst excuse for a road I ever saw. About dark we arrived at a miserable little oasis. There were three ranch houses, lots of kids and dogs, and a tiny log school house with a sheep camp wagon beside it. You may find it hard to believe, but the name of the settlement actually was Lonesome Valley.

The law required a school wherever five kids of school age could be gathered together. Here one family furnished the necessary number of little brains to be cultivated, and here our schoolmarm had come in search of love and adventure.

Since the men were all out on the winter range with the sheep, the three women briefed us on the situation. The schoolmarm had had a baby in the sheep camp where she batched, and had killed it and hid it in an old suitcase. They were pretty mad. It is hard for me to say, however, whether their anger was caused by the death of the baby, or the fact that because nobody had guessed her condition they had been cheated out of a winter's gossip. One old dame did remark that it would have been her first grandchild, for Orley, her seventeen-year-old son, was the papa. Orley had skipped over into Utah on the assumption that the sheriff would come from the opposite direction.

Owing to the hostile atmosphere I suggested that they all go home and get the sheriff some supper. I would be my own nurse as well as doctor. I crawled up into the sheep wagon and shut the door.

A sheep wagon is not a wagon for the comfort of the sheep but a modified version of the covered conveyance you see in the movies being dragged down the mountainside by four galloping horses with a brave young lady sitting beside the driver and taking pot shots at five hundred Indians dashing along behind, who are grabbing their chests and falling from their mounts so fast that one would suppose she had a Buck Rogers special death-ray instead of a Remington carbine which shoots only one bullet at a time. The canvas part of the wagon is built over the wagon box a bit so that a bunk can be placed crossways in the rear and the space under it can be used as clothes closet, food locker and storage for other incidentals. The rest of the wagon is taken up with a sheet-iron stove, a pile of sagebrush or other fuel, a flour sack and a wash basin, while on the wall hangs a piece of broken mirror and a lithograph of several scantily dressed dames.

This one showed the woman's touch in that instead of pieces of harness scattered about there were curtains at the door window, a complete mirror and an orange-crate dressing table. Combs, hair pins, underwear, stockings and other female paraphernalia were tastefully draped over everything.

The patient did not seem to be in desperate shape so I built up the fire and put some water on to heat. This delay gave her a chance to unburden herself to a doctor's more or less sympathetic ear—a procedure that is worth more than all the wonder drugs in most illnesses that affect the female.

She hailed from back East some place. Unlike most of her sex she had more imagination than brains, and had expected to find the West as it was pictured. She had even dreamed for years about handsome cowboys. Her people had objected to her accepting a teaching job so far from home, but she was self-willed and, once she got there, too game to squeal. She got through the first winter as best she could without seeing anybody but the three families of the settlement. Then along in the spring, when even the rabbits and coyotes began to pair off, her natural instincts got the better of her training and good judgment.

The seventeen-year-old sheepherder was her only chance for companionship. As they say about some of the colder countries, in the winter it is too cold to go fishing. Before the summer was out she found that nature had played a trick upon her. She was too crushed to go home, preferring to remain in that hen coop with as little contact with her neighbors as possible.

She had planned to resign in the spring and go into Salt Lake City to hunt up a Florence Crittenden home where she could be taken care of and have her baby adopted. But a few nights before I arrived things had happened so fast that she could remember little of the events that took place.

My examination showed that the infant had been very premature; it probably would have died even if it had been born in a hospital. The mother was in pretty good shape and there was nothing much for me to do but tidy her up a bit and go out and help the sheriff inter the remains. In those days a death certificate was unnecessary when the child was so premature.

I lit the lamp, made her some tea, and opened a can of beans from her larder for my own supper. Then I invited the sheriff in to see her simply as an interested friend and not as a law officer.

I had briefed him on the story before he saw her, and, as he was by nature a kindly old Mormon with a house full of daughters of his own, he was all sympathy. Wanting to be as helpful as possible, he offered to go back to Wendover and apprehend the fleeing Romeo. He would scare him into coming home, where the sheriff, who was a Mormon Elder, could perform a marriage ceremony and make an honest woman of her.

She hooted at the idea. "I would rather be a ruined old maid than married to Orley," she said, and went on to hint that she didn't think Orley had all the marbles he was supposed to have in his head.

This floored the old man. Before he could stop to think he blurted out: "If you felt that way about him, how could you allow yourself to be exposed to these possibilities?"

She looked him straight in the eye for a minute as though searching for an understanding thread. Then, her eyes filling up with tears, she replied with another question: "Mr. Sheriff, did you ever spend a winter in Lonesome Valley?"

Being young and inclined toward the behavior of a jack-ass, I naturally began to bray. Laughs came easy for me in those days, and she sure had the old man on the witness stand where he could not hide behind the Fifth Amendment.

He rubbed his own eyes for a minute and, ignoring my actions, replied: "Yes, I have. In fact, most everybody has a Lonesome Valley hidden some place in his life. It caught up with you pretty young and will overtake the doctor some time. The question before the house now is how can we get you out of it with as few enduring scars as possible?"

That night he and I slept in the schoolhouse. At daybreak we loaded the schoolmarm and her few belongings into the back seat of my old Ford and took her to Wendover. From there the sheriff took her on a train to Salt Lake City and placed her in a nursing home until she was well enough to return to her people.

I left them at Wendover and caught a work train to the track camp, thankful for once that I was again in a society where the only distaff representatives had long ears and said *he-haw* as a good morning greeting. If I ever knew the schoolmarm's name I have long ago forgotten it, along with her appearance and home state, but I will never forget what she said to the sheriff. To me, it shares honors with "There but for the grace of God go I" for being one of the most expressive sentences in our language. In after years I repeated it many times to irate parents, husbands and wives. St. Matthew put it better in "Judge not, that ye be not judged"; but he was not sick and alone in a sheep wagon on a barren Nevada hillside in January.

We were making progress with the railroad across the flat desert, even though shortly after the last snow storm passed, a flash flood caused thirty-five washouts of the track in fifteen miles. There was water everywhere, none of which was fit to use in any way because of the salt.

The next strip of construction was to be along the base of Dutch Mountain, as we had to get some altitude to reach Gold Hill, which was about a thousand feet above the elevation of the salt flats. Like the cloudbursts in summer, the chinooks in winter made the water pour off that old bare mountain like water off a tin roof. Before we got into Gold Hill wash and had clear sailing again we had to contend with many previously dry water-courses, about fifteen fills and an equal number of cuts. Each fill had to have a culvert in the bottom. These culverts had been made by an independent contractor; they were nothing more than boxes of heavy timber twenty feet long and about three feet wide.

In January the chief engineer came to Salt Springs and asked me to drive him up to the construction so that he could look over the proposed right of way before the work crews reached it. As usual some mix-up had occurred. The sub-contractor had delivered the culvert boxes to the stakes listed upon the blueprints as the place for them—or at least he swore he had. But every last culvert was sitting on top of the ridge instead of in the gulley where it was to be used. They could not be rolled down because of the big rocks, so the job had to be done all over again.

But the jack rabbits had taken advantage of the error. Rabbits like to run in the snow on moonlight nights. For safety's sake they travel the ridges so that they can avoid the coyotes hiding behind the rocks on the slopes, and they appreciated the shelter of the culverts. The first one we examined looked as though all the rabbits in the country had taken advantage of it; at each end their tracks fanned out like a railroad freight yard. Since I was a boy I had known that one rabbit can make a lot of tracks in the snow, but here there were millions.

The old man stood and looked at these tracks for a minute or so. Then he turned to me and, removing his cap, made the following oration: "Doctor, you are now seeing something that will go down in history along with the story of the man who pulled the thorn from the lion's paw. Rich and money-mad captains of industry are building a railroad here to rob the earth of her precious metals, yet are so kind-hearted and so sympathetic with the hard lot of the little wild things that they plan underpasses for the rabbits so that they won't be crushed as the whizzing locomotives rush over the rails bearing the ore to the markets of men. It is hardly believable; I have been building railroads for forty years and I never before saw such consideration for our little animal friends."

I reminded him of the fact that no locomotive engineer

would whiz over this track at more than ten miles an hour and that a blind rabbit with arthritis could run rings around the train any time.

"That is just the point," he said. "The rabbit skips ahead of the train for a while. Then, as in the fable of the hare and the tortoise, the hare lies down and goes to sleep. A Deep Creek locomotive creeps up and crushes out his gay spirit and all the other rabbits go into mourning."

Then he put on his cap and began to swear. He was still at it when he left on the work train for Wendover headquarters.

When work actually started on this new section my time was taken up with different types of injuries—rock dust in the eyes of the drillers, banged-up wrists of the men who held the drills, damage caused by flying rocks from the blastings which were liable to clip anybody or anything.

To be near this more hazardous work I moved once more to a tent camp in Gold Hill Canyon. There at last I found a classless society. The hammer men swung the double jacks for a while and then held the drills for the other men to hit while making holes in the rock for dynamite blasting. After the blast they all grabbed shovels and mucked the breakage into dump cars, while well trained mules stood by ready to drag the car to the dump, jump out of the way and let it spill its contents, and drag it back again without benefit of mule skinner.

These men were mostly old prospectors and miners. They drank less and fought less than the track gangs, and were more interested in what a blast would reveal than in Mamie's wares at Wendover.

The General Superintendent and I were standing on the bank one day watching the muckers clean up after a shot in a particularly clear white quartz stratum. He reached into his pocket and drew forth a beautiful piece of Cripple Creek ore. It had gold showing all through the quartz, which looked much like that which the men were loading.

"Go down and speak to Larry," he said to me. "Direct his attention to something and then let this specimen slide down your pants leg and come back here and watch."

In two minutes I had done so and returned to the bank to keep an eye on Larry. He plunged his shovel into the pile of rocks, stooped to get a good hold on the handle, and got it half in the air when he stopped as though he had been shot. Carefully he lowered the load to the ground. Then he straightened up and began fussing with his handkerchief as though he had something in his eye. After looking cautiously around for a minute he dropped his handkerchief to the ground beside the shovel, casually picked it up and that pocket-piece of Cripple Creek ore along with it.

Nothing was said and pretty soon we moved on down the cut.

At supper that night there was excitement in the air. Afterward the men huddled in groups out of earshot of camp and seemed to be in a big argument about something. As soon as it got dark, Dutch Mountain blossomed with moving lanterns as though a flock of lightning bugs had been liberated there. Not a miner was to be seen in camp.

That old rock pile had been pawed over by prospectors for a generation and no ore of value discovered, but most of the men put in night shifts that week developing their claims. Pretty soon I began to worry. Suppose somebody did find a streak of pay rock and, as a result, claims went skyward in price?

I wanted to make a pile all at once too, so even I sneaked off with a flash light. After climbing a half hour I built a little stone monument and so staked a claim.

The boss and I were afraid to ask about his keepsake, but one of the foremen got a look at it and told Larry it was the big man's pocket-piece. That night there was a grand fight between Larry and another old-time miner, who had claimed all the time that the find was plain old Cripple Creek ore.

Larry and his hopeful friends had cursed him roundly, and now they resented his bragging.

When I told the boss about my foolish trip to the mountain, he blushed. "As a matter of fact," he said, "I did the same damned fool thing."

The search for gold is the most entertaining and hopeful occupation on earth, and it makes all men silly if they are not already in that pleasant state.

This was the last camp. Soon the rails were laid and the canyon awoke to the strange sound of locomotive whistles. My friends began scattering to the ends of the earth, wherever construction jobs were to be found.

As this phase of my adventure drew to a close, I began to wonder just what I had gained from it.

First, I had paid off all of my school debts and accumulated a little nest egg to start me off again in practice. I had lost no men from sickness or accident, and because of beginner's luck had avoided any epidemics which might have cut down my earnings through hospital bills.

Second, I had acquired a fondness and respect for the lower third on the scale of life's classifications. Whether unfortunately or not, I never again developed much sympathy with those in the upper brackets of the payroll aristocracy. They do not need it.

Third, I developed a forceful manner of speaking which served me well in the Army, where I was supposed to teach fat old doctors and dumb medical corpsmen how to pitch hospital tents, and which foot was their left one while they learned to march in training camp at Fort Riley, Kansas.

This habit has clung to me. In times of stress I have been known to indulge in language not proper for the drawing room or the bedside. It was indeed fortunate that I chose to practice my profession among such tolerant folks as the Mormons. Outbursts like mine were not allowed them, but they overlooked my lapses and at times, I suspect, envied me this method of lowering my steam pressure.

One good Brother told me that he overheard some Sisters gossiping at his house one day. One lady said: "I like the doctor, but I wish he would be more careful of his language and his pipe. We teach our children to avoid such things, and when they see and hear him it sets them a bad example."

Another old lady, who was also a midwife, replied: "Well, there are a lot of ways of praying and sometimes I think his is more likely to get quick results than our own mild-mannered supplications. I know one thing, when he begins to kick chairs and cuss I silently add an Amen because I know something is about to happen. That is not always the case with a minister."

Oh well, every year of our lives adds something and takes away something. Once we get to see the balance sheet, it is too late to do anything about it.

I bade my friends at the construction camp goodbye one by one, and moved on to become a responsible citizen of a somewhat more respectable society in a boom mining camp.

5

Origins of the Species

The first time I saw Gold Hill, in 1916, it consisted of two buildings and the ruined head-frame of the old Cain Springs Gold Mine. Two families made up the population of the town proper: Jack Hudson lived in the old Cain Springs Boarding House; over on the other side of the flats the Gersters had a little house made of old timbers from the mine heading.

The flat was "patented" ground. Jake Gerster had done enough prospecting upon it to warrant the government's giving him title to the whole area. It consisted of about thirty acres of reasonably level earth, bounded on the west and the north by the Gold Hill wash, or stream bed, and completely surrounded by dry, rocky hills whose ugliness was modified only by a few junipers and shad scale bushes. So spotted over was it with mine shafts and dumps that it looked as though some ambitious gophers had been working there. There was a spring of sorts about a mile above the place, but the water had only wetness to recommend it; it contained so much mineral that it was totally unfit for human consumption unless one's alimentary tract were lined with copper and one's kidneys modeled after stone crushers. The burros liked it, but they could get fat on tin cans and glass bottles, and so were no guarantee of its palatability.

Gold Hill was unique in that it went through three periods of boom and bust instead of the usual single flash of greatness and then oblivion. Twenty-five years before the time of which I write, it was a booming gold camp. In my day the golden fleece had turned to copper. Twenty years later the mining of arsenic blew new life and hope into the discouraged breasts of those who had been too poor to leave when the other booms fizzled out. None of these periods of hope and promise lasted more than three years.

Six weeks after my first visit there were fifty men working in the newly opened copper mines. By the time I had moved there, in the spring of 1917, there were three store buildings, a gasoline pump, the framework for a pool hall, and possibly twenty tent-houses.

Gerster had laid out a townsite. He had named the streets and even gone so far as to reserve plots for a school, a church and a public library. The last two tracts were never used. The school was completed just as the children's parents decided to try their luck elsewhere.

Sanitation was no problem whatever, and so I was spared the grief and troubles of doctors in such new communities. All those old mine shafts, most of which were from fifty to seventy feet deep, were available for the disposal of refuse. The new inhabitants built outhouses over them and were not bothered a particle by the fact that their sanitary facility might be situated right in the middle of the main street.

These structures added a bit of sportiveness to night driving, but they covered up the holes and served in place of numbers to locate dwelling places. If a newcomer stopped you and asked where he could find John Jones's residence, you told him to drive to the third outhouse up Main Street, turn left past two more, and there he would be.

After a big real estate operator arrived in town and built a subdivision on Nob Hill consisting of two shacks eighteen feet by ten, I rented one and the storekeeper rented the other. We paid rent of a dollar a running foot; figuring the area in square feet was too much arithmetic for the landlord-builder.

Because of my connection with the construction camps, I was more fortunately situated than the rest of the inhabitants in that I could take my water keg down to the camp and fill it with Wendover water from the locomotive tank. The rest had to drive twenty-five miles westward over the mountains to Ibapah for their supply. If you felt the absolute necessity of getting wet all over when bathing, you could drive forty miles north to Salt Springs and bathe in Blue Lake, a beautiful little acre of water three to ten feet deep, with a gravel bottom and a constant temperature both summer and winter of seventy-five degrees. Blue Lake's only drawback was the mosquitoes which made you dress quickly once you were out of the water.

If you felt the urge to "get out," you could always drive sixty-five miles north from Gold Hill to Wendover and eat at the railway lunch counter. Its pies were beautiful to look at, but had little else to recommend them.

In fact, one of the most remarkable things about Gold Hill was its inaccessibility. Forty miles to the east was Callao, a metropolis of twenty people. Ibapah was a collection of half a dozen cattle ranches. Fifteen miles beyond it was an Indian Reservation populated by two hundred Gosiutes and three whites. The connecting roads were confined to the beds of the water courses. In time of rain these became raging torrents, but they were dry and sandy most of the year.

South along the stream bed from Gold Hill was Clifton Flats, a mesa-like triangle on top of the Clifton range. This miserable little scrap of ground, covered with shad scale and infested with rattlesnakes, had once been the crossroads of the West. The Overland Trail reached it from the salt desert to the east via the Overland wash, and left it by another dry wash for the Nevada mines and California. If the going got tough on the Humboldt Trail, wagon trains would come south to the Overland, or the Overland travelers could turn north here to the Humboldt.

There was not a tree in the vicinity that an active man could not jump over. The summer traveler in these parts was made to realize the beauty of the Biblical passage about the shadow of a great rock in a weary land. But there wasn't even a rock bigger than a wheelbarrow on the flats, so shade was just not to be had.

Early in my stay on the desert Mr. Johnson, the storekeeper at Wendover, had drawn me a map of the region and taught me the principles of desert navigation. One steered by three landmarks. The first of these was a lofty and lonesome peak called Pilot. All early expeditions over the Humboldt Trail to California were guided by this natural signpost. The second was the Ibapah range, the slopes of which had the unusual distinction of being covered with pine, maple and aspen timber, and which culminated in a peak thirteen thousand feet high. This was used as a marker by the stagecoach and pony express pathfinders on the more southern route to the Pacific.

In the southeast was another noble pile of rocks which were mostly granite. Naturally this was called Granite Mountain. It was a tricky devil. In the glare of the summer sun it was likely to take off and stand on end, or even float up into the sky like a soft gray cloud. The acrobatics performed by this old mountain when the mirage was on probably caused more men to think about swearing off alcohol than any fire-breathing evangelist. When one sees what yesterday was an uncommonly huge and ugly mountain suddenly assume the shape of a flower-filled vase, one is likely to blame it upon something he has taken internally.

Gold Hill was little more than a collection of people gathered together because of a common interest but mostly devoted to their own particular problems. They were about as stable as a bunch of tumbleweeds in a windstorm. Always ready to pull up stakes, they would move on at the first rumor of a metal strike anywhere within traveling distance.

Consequently no one did anything to beautify his surroundings. No one brought anything with him except the bare necessities of life, and never tried to acquire anything that could not be abandoned if he was struck with the notion to move on. It was the custom when a mining camp was deserted for the population to leave everything behind, even the dishes on their tables and the glasses on the bar of the saloon. When a Westerner was preparing to seek a new location, he merely said: "Spit on the fire and call the dog, and let's be off to greener pastures."

A tent or a tent-house was the accepted style of dwelling. Some folks shoveled gravel around the bottom of these structures to keep the snakes from crawling in to get warm, and others bought lumber and built floors. This extravagance, however, was frowned upon. A wood floor required sweeping, but when a dirt floor got too messy all anyone needed to do was move his tent.

It was a classless society. None of the wives had anything for the other women to envy, and as a result few husbands were badgered into going into debt for things they could not afford. Almost every day the women would gather at Mrs. Gerster's to knit impossible sweaters and odd-shaped socks for the soldiers who were freezing in camps around the country because the Army had forgotten that new recruits need clothes, and had not ordered any. The men worked in the mines and prospects. When they were not busy they collected around the stove in the general store to tell tall tales of their experiences in other mining camps, or plan practical jokes to play on one another. It was hard to kill time when no one was interested in going hunting or fishing.

A greenhorn from the East was manna to these starving jokesmiths. One morning when several of us were eating breakfast in George Newcomb's restaurant, two young men entered whose clothes and speech betrayed an unmistakably Eastern origin. They had come out, they said, to look over some of their family's permanent investments held over from a former boom period.

George Newcomb was a wonderful cook and restaurant manager. Though his establishment was only a wooden shed, and the counter a couple of smooth planks, his food was excellent considering what he could get to serve. That morning George had made baking powder biscuits, and to save ingredients had made them very small.

When these were served to the boys from the East, one of them exclaimed: "Oh, look at the dainty little tea biscuits. Imagine finding such things in as crude a place as this!"

Newcomb's usually sunny face grew thunderous. He walked over to Adcock, the storekeeper, and me, and inquired: "How do you bastards like my 'dainty little tea biscuits'?"

"Tea biscuits!" yelled the merchant. "Why, you tight sonofabitch, I thought they were gravy spots. What a place this would be for a cook to start business who wasn't so tight he squeaked when he walked!"

Newcomb reached under the meat block and brought forth a rusty old Navy revolver he had found somewhere. From its looks it might have been lost by Jedediah Smith, the first white man to traverse this region almost a hundred years before, and been left out in the rain ever since. He grabbed it by the barrel and began pounding steak with the butt of the handle, cursing the unappreciative cattle he had to feed, and offering to blow a hole through anyone who answered him back.

His behavior started a bombardment in his direction of hot cakes, spoons, tin cups, and anything else that was loose.

Newcomb reversed his grip on "Old Betsy" and began snapping the trigger as if he meant to kill us all.

The visitors did not wait to see the carnage. They almost tore the door from its hinges trying to get out before the bullets started flying.

Once they were gone, everyone joined in cleaning up. Forever after we called Newcomb "Tea Biscuit George" whenever we wanted to rile him up a bit.

We loved the man, not because of his tea biscuits, but because he made the best griddle cakes any of us had ever eaten. When he first opened he put an empty five-gallon gasoline can on the back of his cooking range, dumped some flour, yeast and other junk into it, and let the mixture ferment for two weeks before he touched it. All the time I knew him he never washed that can inside or out. After breakfast each morning he would just dump in some more flour and stir the mess up a bit. The result was marvelous—golden-brown hot cakes as big as a plate and as light as a feather. Six of them were just an appetizer.

All the women in the camp tried to equal George's mastery of this wonderful breakfast dish, but just as their cakes began to get good they would wash the container, and so spoil it all.

George Newcomb's partner in this business enterprise had once been rich but had lost all his money playing angel for a New York musical comedy. He had the newspaper clippings to prove it. He was typical of our society; its members drifted in from every place and situation in life. The population was never more than a thousand people, including the prospectors out in the hills, but I met men from every corner of the country and from almost every social stratum. Most of them were quite frank about their former experiences, but there were some who had little to say about "what their names were in the states." These characters, of course, interested me most of all. I still wake up at night and wonder about Don Clark and Matt Conklin.

Don Clark and his wife lived in a little tent out on the edge of town and had very little to do with the rest of us. In the morning Don went off to work at the copper mine and at night returned home. He never joined in the town's few social events or in the kidding around the store. His wife had an English accent and left the other women of the camp very much alone. We thought them odd, but paid little attention to them.

The mystery surrounding them appeared later, after I had come home from the Army and settled in Tooele. I found Don working at the smelter. As before, he and his wife were living out on the edge of town and were friendly with none of their neighbors.

One winter Don got sick and could not work. Within a couple of months a man came to my office and asked all about him. I offered to take him to see Don, but he wanted just to be driven by the house. When we got back to the office he gave me a hundred dollars and asked that I watch over this family and see that they were never in need. He also gave me a letter from a big New York bank stating that any bills I might contract in the Clarks' behalf would be paid upon receipt of a statement of service. The only stipulation was that I must cash the checks in Salt Lake City, where I wasn't so well known, and keep my own council about the affair. I had never struck any gold mines in Gold Hill but the old town seemed to be coming through now.

I took good care of Don and his wife, and charged what I fondly thought were New York instead of Utah fees. When Don died I paid for his funeral. The undertaker noised it around that Doc had either gone crazy or was trying to ease his conscience for killing the old man by mistake.

Don's wife soon followed him, and again I had my friend the mortician guessing. He tried to make his bills as modest as possible because I was too crazy to let the county bury her, but it was a good thing he didn't see my expense account.

After it was all over, I wrote the bank and asked to be enlightened on what I had been doing. They answered with a thank-you note and advised that my services had been most satisfactory to their client. That is all I ever knew of the story. I had tried with all my heart to keep those two alive, but that is the way the ball bounces; just when you have a good grip on the hind teat the old cow kicks the bucket.

All I knew about Matt Conklin I learned from Abe Bernstein, who ran a notion store. He advised me to cultivate Matt's acquaintance. Abe had known Matt for years, but was as much in the dark about his past and present as I came to be.

Bernstein, by the way, was a pretty interesting character himself. Years before, he had driven into Tombstone with a wagon full of knickknacks such as old-time peddlers tempted the women folks with—needles, pins, ribbon, false fronts, and such Methodist whisky as Prickley Ash Bitters and Peruna. He was fresh from the old country and knew very little English, but he did so well that he ordered a stock of goods and started a store in Tombstone. Then soon after the stuff arrived, the town took a powder and went off, leaving him bankrupt.

He learned his lesson well. The next thirty years he spent moving from one camp to another, going in with the boom, selling out his stock at a big profit, and waiting to start again until another Eldorado appeared on the horizon. He had prospered and doubtless could have done equally well elsewhere, but he confessed that a big city store scared him. Besides, the desert was in his blood, and so Gold Hill was blessed with his services.

He was a gold mine for an inquisitive youngster like me, and I could always count on him for interesting stories about earlier times. Like a fool I never wrote any of them down. I wasn't spending much time then worrying about how I would be spending my days after seventy. What I was hunting was a bit of Bret Harte romance. I was looking for Tennessee's Partner, or some outcast from Poker Flat. It was twenty years later that I read Mark Twain and discovered that Harte had just followed Dickens' formula for wringing tears out of us human turnips.

Abe Bernstein agreed pretty much with Mamie the hooker about life in the mining camps. He had never seen a six-gun duel and would have taken cover if he had, because, as he said, "Those old Colts would not hit anything the size of a man at a distance of over twenty feet. Nobody but a fool would use one anyhow because there was no need to expose yourself to possible injury when you could hide behind a nice big rock above the trail and pick off your enemy with a thirty-thirty."

There had indeed been killings, but the killer and the victim almost always belonged to the skid row gang of card sharps and thugs and no one cared much what happened to them. When a respectable citizen got in the way and stopped one of their bullets, the trial, conviction and execution of the killer took place all in one day. This efficiency discouraged wrongdoing more effectively than all the lawyers and courts of today. The sheriffs were no braver than any other men, and when business needed tending to, Mr. Sheriff was advised to stay at home.

Bernstein insisted that the great majority of the inhabitants of the boom camps were like our Gold Hill citizens—nice, quiet people who gathered together in town meetings, made their own laws and lived at peace with their neighbors regardless of what they did so long as they did not make too much of a show of their wickedness.

Gold Hill was like that. Utah was supposed to be as dry as laws and officers could make it, but we had a bootlegger in town who just about starved to death because of the nearby competition of the Nevada sagebrush saloons. Prostitution was equally unlawful in the Beehive state, but we had a quiet, nice-looking lady who ran a sex department store in a tent-house over in the next gulch. She never came to town except for mail and groceries and was careful not to recognize any of her customers on these trips. The county sheriff never even heard of her existence until a couple of crazy kids with their heads full of the Wild West moved in on her and got themselves into trouble. The community put up with their nonsense for a time and then decided to give them a talking-to to the effect that if they did not behave, we would run them out.

Bernstein was right about Matt being a character. He was a small, bow-legged, gray-whiskered man who looked somewhat like a ground squirrel. Most people thought him crazy because he had a big sign posted in front of his cabin stating that black-haired women would be shot if they set foot on his property. I thought a lot about this evidence but could come to only one conclusion, that Matt did not like black-haired women. Just why he did not I hoped some day to find out.

Even then there were certain types of the fair sex who set my own teeth on edge. If I had been situated in such a dismal location as Matt's cabin and wanted to live undisturbed, I just might have tried to discourage people I did not like from getting too familiar. If that was insanity it was a mild form of it. There seemed to be no reason for black-haired women to invade this forbidden ground except to test his determination. Should that have been their motive, they deserved to be shot.

Matt lived over on the desert side of Clifton Mountain, about halfway to the summit. The only thing he could see from his picture window was the white salt desert, with Granite Mountain going through its sitting-up exercises whenever the mirages were in order. His dooryard was devoid of soil, and only the usual scattered junipers and shad scale broke the barrenness of the hillside above him. Matt had a dog named Joe. The third member of the household was as surly and uncommunicative as Matt himself, a big male burro that like his owner seemed to shun contact with his kind and never joined the other burros in their frolics about the camp.

Matt had never made a shipment of ore, but he came to town about once a month to get heavy supplies such as sugar, flour and blasting powder. He sent his dog Joe over almost every day to get the mail, smoking tobacco and similar light articles. He had two friends in town: Abe Bernstein and Jake Gerster, the postmaster, who read the notes Matt tied around Joe's neck and went to the store with him to secure the supplies wanted. But Matt was not friendly toward Mrs. Gerster. Her hair was gray, but in twenty years Matt had never said so much as how-do-you-do to her. Being a neighborly soul herself, she was the originator of the idea that he was crazy.

On his infrequent trips to town Matt would purchase a month's supply of bootleg whisky, get pretty well oiled, and then drop in on the storekeeper to play a game of solo or two with him in the back of the store. His friendship with Bernstein had started many years ago in a camp called Calico down Death Valley way, but Matt had never taken the old man into his confidence. When he was well lit up he would entertain the storekeeper by reciting poetry.

Bernstein told me about this habit and suggested that should I see old Joe lying by the store door and Jack the burro standing patiently nearby, I should come into the store and keep my mouth shut and listen to the recital.

A few days later the signs were right, so I walked in to buy a pair of gloves, and stayed to listen. Pretty soon Matt began to quote Robert Service between deals of the cards. From there he took off. The cards were forgotten as he quoted poetry that ranged from Shakespeare's sonnets to Eugene Field. In fact, he quoted from poets and poems that I had never heard of. The drunker he got, the more poetry he spouted. Finally when Matt got to John Keats, Bernstein signaled to me that once he got a grip on "Ode to a Nightingale" the curtain was about to come down. He was going fine until he reached the third stanza:

Fade far away, dissolve, and quite forget
What thou among the leaves hast never known,
The weariness, the fever, and the fret [Matt called it "sweat"]

Here, where men sit and hear each other groan;
Where palsy shakes a few, sad, last gray hairs,
Where youth grows pale, and spectre-thin, and dies;
Where but to think is to be full of sorrow
And leaden-eyed despairs. . . .

When his nightingale had given this last despairing squawk, Matt's head sank down on his chest and he seemed to sleep. I tiptoed out.

A few times after that night I just happened to be in Matt's neighborhood and stopped in for a chat. I did not make much headway in learning more about him. He would talk about rocks, prospects and the evil nature of burros, but I could never steer the conversation around to women or literature. I gave up and limited my neighborliness to old Joe.

Joe was a large brown dog with a coat that denoted collie ancestry. One ear stuck straight up and the other lay useless at the side of his head. Jake Gerster told me that Joe, as his master may have been, was unlucky in his one attempt at a love affair. He had followed a lady coyote home one night, and her irate husband had about torn his ear off. Jake Gerster had helped Matt sew it back on. I never saw Joe taking part in the canine set's occasional romantic parties, so perhaps he too had a No Trespassing sign on his private range.

I had about forgotten Matt until one cold, windy winter midnight when I was returning from a sick call. As I approached the Clifton Range from the salt desert I saw a queer sort of light bobbing about on the side of the mountain. It could be a lantern, I thought, but surely there were no tenderfeet around who would be crazy enough to go hunting snipe in this kind of weather, or natives so hungry for a joke as to take them. I had heard of fox fire but never seen any, so I stopped the car on a little rise to watch this supposedly natural phenomenon.

Then I remembered that in the fall the Dunnions, who

lived in Salt Lake City, had sent a young Italian named Tony
out to the half-cave, half-tent arrangement they maintained
at their mine, about a mile south of Matt, for their men to do
the assessment work necessary for property holders to keep
their title. Tony had called upon me to say that in March his
wife was going to "make a baby." She was too shy to come to
see me herself. I had told Tony to let me know when I was
needed and I would care for her. Perhaps she had been working harder at the project than Tony anticipated and he had
gone to Gold Hill to call me. Having been told where I was,
he might be trying to intercept me before I got into Overland canyon on my way home.

I kept the engine of the car running so that the headlights
would burn—the electricity came from the magneto on those
early Fords—to give him a point to head for. All the while I
waited his coming, I cussed to myself. I was sleepy and cold,
and I did not relish that climb which would be followed by
what a colleague called, "wallowing around a bed all night
trying to help some woman have a baby." In Ecclesiastes
Solomon said, "Better is the end of a thing than the beginning thereof." But this just goes to show that with all his
wives he never was around at the culmination of pregnancy
and did not know what he was talking about.

Pretty soon Joe showed up, barking and prancing around
like a man who is to become a father for the first time and is
overwhelmed by the prospect. He climbed up on the running
board and tugged at my sleeve to tell me as best he could
that his master Matt was in trouble. Matt himself arrived in
a minute or two and confirmed Joe's diagnosis.

As soon as he could catch his breath he gasped, "For God's
sake, Doc, come quick."

"Come where, Matt? Tell me all about it and take your
time."

He coughed, kicked the gravel and turned his back to me.

Then he blurted out: "That Tony has gone to Salt Lake. His wife just came to my place. She is going to have a baby *right in my cabin.* She said so."

Then, half turning, he seemed to be addressing the mountain. "Why persecute thou me? The foxes have holes and the birds of the air have nests and this son of man hath no place to lay his head but what some damned black-haired woman will find it. Is there no help for this widow's son? Must I always be cursed by these fiends from Hell?"

I am ashamed to say that the irony of the situation quite overcame any professional reserve I might have had. I spent the next five minutes rolling around on the ground braying like a drunken jackass.

Matt kept wringing his hands and imploring me to hurry. He had it all figured out. I was to take the little lantern, Joe would guide me, and he would follow us, as he was too tired to keep up. I saw through that ruse. Matt was planning to get lost and stay lost until things quieted down. But this was a first baby; if it followed the natural course of things, we had all night to make that climb. I insisted that he go ahead with the lantern, for I would be loaded down with my obstetrical bag and could not travel very fast either.

Our little procession started the long ascent. Joe kept dashing ahead and rushing back to us, barking as though he were driving a flock of sheep into a pen. Matt stumbled along swinging that smoky coal-oil lantern, his head bowed in either grief, mortification, or general disgust toward the world in general and me in particular, because whenever I thought of a black-haired woman having a baby in this purely masculine retreat I had to giggle. After about an hour's climb we reached Tony's dugout.

Before we started over the ridge between Tony's dugout and Matt's cabin, I suggested we stop and investigate. I was sure that, if it was at all possible, Mrs. Tony would return to her own bed for the blessed event. She was there all right, and so was the baby.

The place was as cold as a polar bear's pocket. I grabbed Matt, and pushed him into the dugout.

"Build the biggest fire you can," I told him. "And heat some rocks in the oven. We can use them for hot water bottles."

Meanwhile I tended to things in the tent room. The baby felt like a fish fresh from a mountain brook. As soon as I had him separated from his former meal ticket I rolled him in a little blanket and rushed into the dugout, where Matt was huddled cosily by the roaring fire. I had intended to lay the kid in an old blasting-powder box and return to care for the mother, but the devil tempted me. I shoved him into Matt's arms.

"Now make yourself useful," I said, "and warm this baby up."

He recoiled as though I had handed him a rattlesnake. But people, I have found, have a way of obeying a doctor in times of emergency. Matt spread his arms, and I placed the babe in them.

Then I hurried back to clean up the bed and get the mother into some dry clothes. When I got there, she was up on her feet, slinging bed clothes every which way. In broken English she gave me to understand that her mother had given her that featherbed and she did not intend to spot it.

I made her understand that I was nurse as well as doctor right now and to get to hell back in there. I would tend to the bed-making.

All this took some little time. Once I was through I started on a trot for the dugout room. But I stopped just inside the door.

My father had been a portrait painter and had spent a deal of time trying to interest me in art, but I would have none of it. I have regretted my attitude only a couple of times in my life, and this was the first one. Perhaps I was not ordained to be an artist, but I had a quick eye for a scene that would touch men's souls. This was one of them. Here was a background of native granite rock walls, log stringers with the bark still on them supporting the low ceiling, some cedar wood and powder boxes piled in the corner for fuel, and the little sheepherder stove doing its best to warm the place and illuminating the picture with the glow from the open fire box. The whole scene was softened by this flickering light. Matt was sitting on a nail keg in the only bright spot, holding that squalling baby close to his breast. At his feet lay Joe, his one good ear pricked up higher than usual at the unaccustomed noise and on his face that expression of sympathy and sorrow which all good dogs assume when their master is sad.

A quick look at Matt explained it. The poor old man was crying. Not audibly, but tears were plainly stealing down his cheeks and making tracks through the dirt thereon, as he sat looking at that baby.

For a minute it seemed that I could see his whole life in retrospect. I imagined that once before he had held in his arms a baby boy that was his own, that my thoughtlessness had opened up some once-healed wound of his spirit, and that he was weeping for what might have been. For once in my life I showed a spark of understanding, and quietly withdrew before he could know that I had seen his shame and hopelessness.

I waited a minute and then called loudly, "I'll be right there, Matt."

By the time I re-entered, the spell was gone. He had wiped his eyes and was trying to balance the baby and cut a chaw of plug tobacco at the same time.

I wrapped the babe in some warm dry clothes and put the hot rocks into the powder box and tucked the child in with them. Now it was time to nourish the actors. Matt put on a pot of coffee. I hunted around until I found a can of beans and dumped them into a frying pan to heat. First we gave the mother a cup of hot coffee generously spiked with "vino," and the baby a few spoonfuls of warm water. Then Matt and I sat down to kill the rest of the grape juice, the coffee and the beans. Joe licked the dishes and finished the beans. At last everybody was calm again.

It was still an hour or two until daylight, so we lit our pipes and settled down to being night nurses in this obstetrical ward. We talked of many things, but I was careful not to mention anything that might tempt Matt to tell me of things which were, I now knew, so painful to him.

After I went off to war I never saw Matt again, but Mrs. Gerster told me that he grew very fond of little Tony and was often seen baby-sitting for the parents when they were busy. I hope that there is a hereafter where Matt and that other black-haired baby can be united and recognize their relationship and enjoy that communion so precious to a father and his son.

6

Our James Gang

The Deep Creek Cannon Ball was truly a limited express. Because of the poor roadbed she could not exceed a speed of fifteen miles per hour. The grades held her pay load down to three boxcars and the all-purpose passenger car which I had met at the beginning of this adventure.

The Cannon Ball was supposed to leave Wendover at three o'clock in the morning, providing the Western Pacific was on time from Salt Lake City, and to arrive at Gold Hill at nine A.M. Going downhill, she could do a little better. She left Gold Hill at ten A.M., arriving at Wendover at one P.M. in time to connect with the eastbound passenger train on the main line.

It was not uncommon for Gold Hill hunters to ride down to Salt Springs on some passing truck and stay there for the evening flight of ducks, when the birds would roost on the ponds. In the morning they would flag the train for a ride back home. So the engineer thought little of it when a lantern was swung across the tracks as he approached Salt Springs before daybreak on an April morning.

The following account of what happened was given me by the head brakeman, who was shooting craps with the fireman in the gangway of the locomotive tender when the signal was flashed.

Two men approached out of the darkness and shot off their revolvers a couple of times. Then, pulling handkerchiefs up over their faces, they announced that this was a stickup.

The engineer replied: "Cut out your damned clowning and climb aboard. We are already late."

The leader yelled back: "Honest, this is a stickup. We mean business." He flourished his gun in the air.

Still unconvinced, the "hog head" retorted: "Well, get on with your robbing, then. It will be light enough for the mosquitoes to find us in a few minutes, and I'd rather be shot than sit here then. I'll give you five minutes."

The bandits consulted together. The leader replied, "But you must uncouple the engine and run down the track a way while we go through the passengers."

"I belong to the enginemen's union," said the engineer, "and am not supposed to uncouple cars. Do it yourselves."

So the second bandit crawled in behind the tender and broke the coupling.

By this time the conductor had arrived. When informed of the delay, he began to whoop and laugh. He was a large fat man, and like Saint Nick's in the poem, his belly shook like a bowlful of jelly. That is, it did until a bandit stuck a gun against it. Then the conductor scrambled back aboard the passenger car, yelling: "Hide your money! Some idiots are holding us up."

The passengers quickly followed his advice and began stowing their valuables behind the seat cushions.

The bandits' entire haul amounted to about three dollars and the conductor's watch, which was of the dollar variety and ticked so loudly you could hear it above the rattle of the train in motion. There was no cargo except a bunch of bananas. The robber picked off a pocketful of the ripest, grabbed the mail sack and yelled to his companion, who was guarding the crew and passengers with a cocked gun, to come on. Then he jumped from the train.

The second man tried to slip his six-gun back into its holster, but he forgot to lower the hammer. The thing went off, and the bullet struck a passenger in the leg. The bandit dropped his gun on the floor, and tore out after his departed partner.

The train crew decided they had better return to Wendover to report the incident and put the wounded man on a freight train that was about due to leave for Salt Lake City. Afterward they resumed their journey to Gold Hill.

It was not unusual for them to be late, but when they arrived in Gold Hill and reported the holdup, everybody was interested.

Four of us started out in an automobile to the scene of the crime to look for clues. We found some before we had traveled five miles. The garage man was one of our number. After watching the dust in the road a bit, he asked the driver to stop. He got out and walked ahead for a few feet. Then he announced that the Rover Boys who had moved in on our local madam had been down this way and back since last night. There were not more than a dozen cars in town, all the tires of which had lost their treads on the rocks long ago. But here was the imprint of a brand new diamond-tread tire plainly outlined in the dirt. It had apparently been mounted upon the right rear wheel.

The night before, he told us, the bandits, probably wanting to be sure of a safe getaway, had purchased a new Goodyear diamond-tread from him. He had mounted it on their right rear wheel. That was their one slip in an otherwise perfect crime.

We drove on to Salt Springs and got out to look the ground over. Sure enough, the car bearing this tell-tale tire had been pulled off the road and stopped behind a big rock a short way from the Salt Springs siding. We could plainly see where the car had backed around and returned toward Gold Hill. To make the evidence more damning, there were some banana skins lying close by. Next, one of the fellows who had wandered off a bit yelled, "There is some new kind of rattlesnake in this sagebrush." Investigation showed the conductor's watch ticking merrily away in the bush where the bandits had evidently thrown it.

We swore one another to secrecy, but by the time we had been home an hour even the burros knew who had done it. Nobody bothered mentioning it to the culprits, however, and we decided to await the coming of the sheriff and the postal inspector, who were to arrive that evening by car.

As soon as they had been briefed upon our evidence they formed a posse and deputized all the able-bodied men in town to surround the tent-house in the canyon, which had a certain reputation, and demand the surrender of the guilty parties. But Gold Hill showed her independence and good sense. We refused to be sworn in as deputies.

The grocery store proprietor, who was somewhat the unofficial mayor of the community and spokesman for its inhabitants, expressed our sentiments. "Now listen, Mr. Sheriff," he said, "we do not intend to help you make headlines and we are not going to be sworn in as deputies. Gold Hill does not want to go down in history as the second battle of the O.K. Corral because none of us cares to be shot at by a bunch of crazy kids.

"Besides, Daisy, the mistress of that establishment, is a nice quiet little hooker, a standout in her profession, who has many friends and patrons in this gathering right here. She is a good customer of this store and pays her bills promptly. I for one don't want to see her hurt, and she might be if you turn this bunch loose with license to shoot at her place of business. If you want those kids, just you sit there on your big fanny, and when they come into the store I'll personally conduct them back here and you can arrest them without getting up.

"Gold Hill is a peaceful community and we all vote. You had better listen to us and do it the easy way."

Some wag piped up: "I'll tell you what to do, Mr. Sheriff. Just deputize the wives, they will be glad to do your shooting for you. Daisy has the prettiest ankles in town and all the girls despise her whether they have reason or not."

What could the poor sheriff do but wait? He didn't have much of that to do, for within an hour one of the boys came to town for some tobacco. The store manager took him back and made him acquainted with the law. The other bandit was waiting in their car. The sheriff just walked to its door and arrested him.

The two kids left us that night, handcuffed together like real criminals. They looked like a couple of youngsters who had been caught throwing spitballs in school and were going to see the principal. They were lodged in the Tooele County jail until their trial. They said Daisy had warned them about monkeying with Uncle Sam, and they had hidden the mailsack out in the sagebrush. They served their time in the state penitentiary.

I knew one of them in after years; he was as good a citizen as the average, and raised a nice family. What became of the other and of Daisy, I do not know. If the darn fools had just left the mailsack alone and not accidentally shot an innocent passenger, we probably would have given them a good spanking and chased them over the line into Nevada before the law officers arrived. But there are some things that are not just high-spirited antics, and fooling with the mail and shooting people in the legs are among them.

When the mailsack was found, the only damage to its contents had been caused by a family of chipmunks that had taken up residence therein after gnawing a hole in the sack itself. The mail was mostly mail-order catalogues, rolled so tightly and wrapped so securely that even a chipmunk's teeth made little impression upon them.

This was fortunate, because these catalogues filled the void while the world was waiting for television to give people excuses for not reading the Bible and other good books. They had an appeal for everybody in the family: mother pored over

Track-layers going out to work.

The cook tent.

Prospecting with the aid of a sheepherder pony.

Gold Hill as I first saw it, showing the old Cain Springs mine workings.

Gold Hill after it became citified. In the upper right is the pool hall, where we danced.

A youthful doctor and his car, before our tent-bedroom.

Ruth at the back door of our Gold Hill home.

Ruth on a fishing trip to Mount Ibapah.

The result of a good day's fishing.

The builders of the road to Ferber, Nevada, having lunch. At the
far left stand Ruth, Mrs. Gerster, and I.

The Deep Creek Cannon Ball.

Freight depot of the Deep Creek Railroad at Gold Hill.

Nell Murbarger

...andoned freight cars of the Deep ...eek Railroad, Gold Hill.

...e original Cain Springs mine, Gold ...ll.

Nell Murbarger

Nell Murbarger

A dugout cabin at Clifton, Utah, similar to the one Tony inhabited.

Marker on the sight of the Deep Creek
Pony Express station, Ibapah, Utah.

Nell Murbarger

Nell Murbarger

Deserted ranch house near Ibapah

The road between White Horse Pass
and Gold Hill.

Nell Murbarger

An old ranch barn near Ibapah.

Nell Murbar

the beautiful pictures of cookstoves, all black and shiny; daughter admired the dresses and the handsome men modeling latest style suits at ten dollars per suit; the old man panted for the harnesses and farm implements as did the hart after the water-brooks; and the boys planned to save their money and buy some traps to catch some mink or foxes, sell the pelts and buy a real gun. When the old folks were not looking, the boys would turn to the section which showed ladies parading around in long underwear, and sit and admire and sweat and blush and wonder why such revealing pictures should be so attractive.

If my memory is correct, I first realized that women have legs while thumbing through one of these catalogues, a discovery which still interests me though TV has taken the romance out of the spectacle. Somehow the dancers on the screen remind me of particularly active spiders. Familiarity breeds contempt, I guess.

The arrival of a new catalogue was an event in Gold Hill homes as well as in all other isolated communities. Everybody wanted to turn the pages and to dream. Besides, the old one was likely used down to the slick pages in color, and the current issue was badly needed in the little house out back.

7

Love Stories Are Where You Find Them

I was getting along into my thirties. If I did not get married pretty soon, I knew, I would be so fixed in my ways that no woman could ever live with me. I had seen enough male old maids to know I did not want to grow like them.

Love was not exactly a stranger to me. The women in the picture, however, were much better than I was. Unfortunately, they knew it. They were bent upon banishing my bad habits and remaking me into the ideal husband they had dreamed about. Their plans might have worked out, but they were so anxious to get on with the job that they started in on it before they had any legal claims upon me. Somehow I wanted a wife who would know right away that I was just about what the doctor ordered, or was smart enough to pretend she did.

I thought I had found a girl in Utah who seemed to be satisfied with me as I was. Because she had two older brothers, who had treated her with the usual lack of consideration due a kid sister, she probably did not expect too much from any other male. She could not cook, she could not sew, and she did not have much money. But she was blessed with that rare feminine charm, a sense of humor. That more than made up for her deficiencies in the more practical matters of married life.

I knew of some women in the mining camp who made life a hell on earth for their husbands because of the casual way of living they discovered in these crude surroundings. I did not want to shipwreck my matrimony on Gold Hill granite.

On the other hand, I was never designed to be a brother in a monastery. The exclusively male society I had experienced these last months had so affected me that even the Indian squaws did not look so repulsive to me as they had appeared when I first saw them. If I was going to get married, now was the time to get on with it.

Mrs. Jake Gerster was the obvious person for me to consult in this affair of the heart.

Before I had settled in Gold Hill I had heard a good deal about Mrs. Gerster from many people. Even Mamie of the Blue Goose had sung her praises. The reports were, I soon discovered, not exaggerated.

She had been raised in pleasant surroundings. As a young girl she had married a rich contractor who delighted in covering her fingers with diamonds and fulfilling her every wish. Then he lost everything on a railroad building project in Colorado. Even his wife's precious diamonds had to be sacrificed to pay his debts.

Jake Gerster then struck out for the new Eldorado in Nevada to rebuild his fortunes. Luck was not with him. Finally he landed in Gold Hill, Utah, where there was a short-lived boom. He refused to let his wife join him there because of his poor prospects and the harsh life of the place.

His wife came anyhow. A train got her as far as Montello, Nevada, about 150 miles northwest of Gold Hill. From there she thumbed a ride on a freight wagon and arrived to surprise him.

For thirty years they lived and struggled on their rock pile. Jake would work down in the shaft, and his wife would man the windlass that brought the waste rock to the surface. After their day's work, they would return home to their jerry-built cabin.

Inside was another world. Mrs. Gerster had sent home for

her furniture, her linen, her china. That house looked like the Beverly-Hilton Hotel to us lonesome guys.

She was always happy to see new faces, and acted as a welcoming committee for all newcomers. She would do what she could to help them get settled in Gold Hill. Whenever any of us was lucky enough to be invited to her house for tea, he dug out a white shirt and a necktie, and cleaned his fingernails.

Mrs. Gerster's biography would be a story of true love and devotion beyond the possibilities of the average person. It would reveal a spirit as brave and gallant as that of any of the female saints.

This time I called upon her, my troubles were not of the kind that a cup of sugar or an extra chair could satisfy. I wanted advice on a more serious subject than how to cook beans in hard water.

Mrs. Gerster quizzed me carefully on the disposition and the past life of my lady. Then after due consideration she advised me to ask the girl her own opinion. She cautioned me to state the facts plainly.

Finally she said: "Well, there is this one thing about it, living in Gold Hill will be a fine test of her devotion. If she loves you enough to put up with this for a year, you can face the future with confidence. If she doesn't, you had better find it out in the beginning than years later when there will be children to consider."

I took her advice. I wrote the letter, stating emphatically that there was only one flower in the region and that was a geranium growing in a pot in Mrs. Gerster's living room. Its dirt had been hauled from Callao, and it was kept alive by water brought from Ibapah.

Ruth's answer was assuring. She wrote that she had spent her childhood in a Nevada mining camp, and her girlhood in Salida, Colorado, which was all railroads and mines. She even suggested that she might know more about mining

camps than I did. At any rate, she would welcome the opportunity of coping with both me and the other hardships.

We planned to meet in Salt Lake City in early April, and
be married there. I could get my car out of storage, and we
could drive back to our honeymoon cottage in Gold Hill.

Ruth had not notified any of her friends of the impending
wedding on the off-chance, I suppose, that I might fail to
show up. I prevailed upon a doctor friend to support me
through the ordeal. An old Presbyterian minister, a lifelong
friend of Ruth's family, tied the knot.

We had planned a quiet dinner together at the hotel. But
some of my medical friends had other ideas; doctors will do
anything to play a joke upon a fellow practitioner. As soon as
we were seated in the dining room, the parade began—wedding cake with a bride and groom on top, and covered with
flowers, white pastry doves and all the other rubbish they and
the hotel chef could think up that would draw attention to a
bridal couple who were trying to act like old married folks.
Then they gathered around the table and sang "Me and My
Gal," a popular hit of the day, over and over again so that
everyone else in the dining room could enjoy watching us
blush and suffer.

Next day Salt Lake City was having one of its most violent April snowstorms. Because of this and the roads, which
were bad enough anyway, we had to detour to southern
Utah and then head north along the Nevada line for three
hundred miles.

The only map we had was one a sheepherder had drawn
for us on an old envelope. He was facing south when he did
it, and did not allow for the fact that we would be traveling
north. Before we realized that his directions were reversed,
we got lost several times.

We saw only one human habitation, and just as we got to
it, the car broke down.

In a moment of absent-mindedness I had invited Ruth's

brother to accompany us. This gesture had conflicted with Ruth's ideas of a honeymoon trip, but I certainly was glad he was along when the car gave out. He was a much better mechanic than I.

At ten P.M. the third night we finally arrived at Gold Hill.

No one had told me about the mining camp tradition concerning the first bride to arrive. In some way it must have been derived from ancient fertility rites, for the miners believed the degree of welcome they bestowed upon a new bride would be reflected in the richness of the ore bodies they found. Gold Hill needed some pretty strong medicine of that variety.

As soon as I had left town they took over the pool hall, and stored the tables. Then they sent a truck 150 miles to Ely, Nevada, for a piano, and scoured the country for a couple of old fiddlers. They prepared several washtubs of sandwiches and boilers of coffee. They also bought out the entire stock of a Nevada sagebrush saloon.

After all this preparation there was still some money left in the fund they had collected for the celebration. So they sent to Salt Lake City for an enormous linen tablecloth and linen napkins as a gift for the bride. As it turned out, we used the napkins for tablecloths, and stored the cloth itself. It was big enough to cover our entire house. Ruth had to take it outdoors to unfold it completely.

Some ladies were waiting at the cabin to greet the bride. Without giving her time even to powder her face they rushed her over to the dance at the pool hall. That was the last I saw of her until the dance broke up at eight o'clock next morning. She had danced every dance with miners and prospectors in their hobnailed boots and her feet were well trampled.

We sneaked over to the Greasy Spoon for some of Newcomb's sourdough hot cakes and then home to bed. But no

The place was inhabited by a half-dozen whiskery old prospectors who had failed to get to the dance. They were not taking any chances with their luck by neglecting to call upon the bride. As these retired, others took their place. We did not get our luggage unpacked for days. There were prospectors around all day and we were too dog-tired to unpack at night.

The welcome kept up for two weeks. Every one of the prospectors brought Ruth a box of candy. The store had only a dozen boxes of ancient chocolates on hand. As soon as the supply was exhausted the store would send a boy to collect the gifts so that they might be sold over again. We got credit for the merchandise returned.

One particularly loud specimen was heartshaped and decorated with an enormous bow of red ribbon. It made ten round trips. Finally a United States senator arrived in town to look over some of his permanent investments. Like the rest of the prospectors he bought a box of candy to present to the bride in the hope that luck might send him a sucker on whom he could unload his findings. It was the heartshaped one. That time we kept the box. Ruth insisted that she might never again receive a present from such a distinguished man as Senator Reed Smoot.

The valentine kicked around for a while until finally it was fed to a hungry burro who enjoyed eating the red ribbon as much as the candy.

Ruth classified her visitors quickly. She showed real affection for the poor old beat-up prospectors, but she insisted that the younger men were just fooling around the mountains to keep away from their wives and were enjoying this relief from domesticity.

The old boys adopted Ruth as the long-lost daughter they never had. Some of them were pretty handy. They exercised their talents in making Ruth a dressing table and chests of drawers out of discarded dry goods boxes. They made so many that I had to build a tent-house so that we would have some place to sleep.

Ruth never complained of her visitors until a delegation of squaws dropped in one day and sat the whole afternoon without uttering a word except a grunt when she addressed them. That was an Indian's way. The time came, however, when they would gossip with her like a flock of hens.

Once the human visitors dwindled, the animal population took over. I discovered that my new wife attracted dogs, burros and other quadrupeds as a trumpet vine does humming-birds. A beautiful big English setter who loved me when I had a shotgun in my hands and hated me when I didn't arrived each day after breakfast and stayed until dark unless his owner or I went hunting. A six-foot long dog lying on the floor of an eight-foot room does not leave much space for mobility.

The burros and a neighbor's pet pig got there about as early as the dog and brayed and grunted until Ruth fed them some of her culinary mistakes. If there were none, the jack-asses lunched upon the clothes on the line or nibbled the top of my Ford roadster. Anything he could chew was food for a burro. The wrappers on empty fruit cans were a treat for them. In the evening a horned toad came and sat on the door-step, patiently waiting for Ruth to use the fly swatter to furnish his supper. Matt's old dog Joe, who came over the hill for his master's supplies every day or so, always stopped for a visit on his way home. He was a smart dog. Whenever the basket he carried in his mouth was heavy laden he would wait for either Ruth or me to carry it for him to the summit of the hill.

Mrs. Gerster watched over us like a hen with two chicks. She was an ever-willing teacher of the science of housekeeping in a desert cabin.

I suppose every new bride faces the same general problem

such as getting acquainted with the man she has married, meeting his friends and trying to make a favorable impression upon them so that they will not think "dear old John got took," and staying clear of her new mother-in-law. But the girl who marries a small-town doctor has to face a lot more serious situations than her sisters who marry men of other professions. And if her new home is in a small isolated mining camp, man, she has had it.

In the first place, all of the older ladies of the community elect themselves honorary mothers-in-law. They advise her how to care for her spouse and feel free to discuss her deficiencies with one another and relay the conclusions to her. In a mining camp everybody knows everybody else's business. A new bride is better than a best-selling sex novel as a subject of conversation.

Ruth was lucky in one respect; there were not many older ladies to advise her. Due to the great number of lonesome old prospectors, I acquired a collection of male mothers-in-law and she collected dividends from their fatherly concern long after she had forgotten their names.

Something happened on the very first day we were in our new home that she used to great advantage for the next forty years. The first delegation of whiskery old prospectors had just left our house. Ruth's feet were about killing her because of the hobnailed boots that had trampled on them at the dance the night before. She got out a wash pan and decided to bathe them in hot water to ease the bruises and bumps.

Mrs. Gerster had told her that she would be over in the morning to wise her up on some wifely chores. When Ruth heard a gentle knock on the door, she shoved the pan under the kitchen cabinet and went to welcome her. But what she greeted in her bare feet was another delegation of prospectors, bearing gifts for the new bride.

Ruth had been taught never to make excuses for her appearance. If visitors did not like it they could always leave.

So she sat and visited with them for a pleasant half hour, and they took their departure without mentioning her overly pink tootsies.

But one of the prospectors went straight to the storekeeper and asked him to insist that I buy my wife a pair of shoes.

"Why," he said, "the poor girl's feet were all red and swollen already from walking over these rocks and cactuses. It just ain't fitting that the doc should let his wife run barefoot when even the squaws wear moccasins."

I thought it a huge joke when I heard about it, but the time was to come when I would have gladly murdered that old miner. In after years when Ruth thought her allowance inadequate, she did not howl about it. She just went about her household chores barefooted. I got the hint.

Ruth says she doesn't mind giving away trade secrets now that we are both too old to worry about such things, but she claims that for forty years she has had to use the indirect method of getting her way. She has also said she knew when she married me that my disposition was somewhat like that of a rancher's old herd bull down in the country where she was raised. The rancher would say: "Why, that old bull is as gentle as a kitten. Even my grandchildren lead him around and ride him to water. But when he begins to bellow and paw the dirt, we just stay out of the pasture. In five minutes he gets so interested in seeing how far he can paw that dirt he forgets what he was bellowing about and calms down as quick as he started."

The launching of the matrimonial bark, like that of any other ship, is only the beginning. The subsequent shakedown cruise or honeymoon is bound to reveal some unexpected flaws in the design and construction, as well as differences of opinion among the crew as to their duties and privileges. The quicker these differences are recognized and settled, the sooner the ship begins to sail a straight course. Most couples are inclined to avoid honeymoon fights, but they are to be hoped for.

Just before we started to drive to Ibapah one morning I hung the ever-present and most necessary water bag on a hook on the frame of the windshield on my wife's side of the car. The top of the roadster was down. I asked Ruth to watch that the water bag did not jar off as I expected to pour the contents into the radiator when we reached the summit of the canyon. The old car always boiled like a tea kettle before it reached Clifton Flats. I could refill the bag at the Sheridans' in Ibapah.

I suppose Ruth let her eyes wander and was admiring the view or her new husband. At any rate, when we reached the top, the bag was gone.

It didn't make too much difference as the road was all downhill to our destination. Nevertheless I spent the trip down lecturing her upon the fact that now she too had responsibilities and was not just taking a ride with her best beau. From then on what was mine was also hers to use and to take care of. I guess I laid it on a bit.

Before we got to the Sheridans' we ran into a spot where the irrigation ditch had overflowed onto the road. We got stuck in the mud.

Ruth was dolled up in a new mustard-colored suit. Mustard was the color that spring. Her suit looked as though it had just dripped off a hot dog. I hated anything yellow on her, as her color was blue, and she knew as well as I did that she looked better in it. Even then women would have painted themselves like barber poles if that were the style.

The car failed to pull out of the mud. The radiator sounded as if it would blow up any minute. I thought I should release the cap so that the steam could escape a little. I meant just to give it a turn, but the steam tore it from my hand and the entire contents of the radiator—rusty water, corn meal, soap and everything recommended to stop leaks—rose like a geyser into the air. It went up about ten feet and curved downward. Every drop landed on Ruth's new suit.

Ruth left that car like a scared cat and did not stop running until she was fifty feet away. Then she sat down and buried her face in her hands. She looked so forlorn that I rushed up to tell her how sorry I was. For a minute she paid no attention to me. Then she raised her head and delivered a statement of policy for which I have ever since been glad.

"I know what the matter is," she said, "you are tired of being married already. You thought that if you spoiled my new suit some way I would get mad and go home. Well, Mister, you are talking to the wrong girl. I promised to live with you until death parts us, and I intend to do just that. No matter how unreasonable you are or what you do, you are stuck with me from now on."

What could a guy do but gather her in his arms and promise almost anything?

It all wound up in a compromise. Ruth bought a new water bag with her own money, and I bought her a new suit. The water bag cost one dollar fifty and the suit forty. This, I think, is about par for the course when a man and his wife decide to share and share alike. The new suit was blue.

I expect that if Ruth had known that day by the Ibapah mudhole what was in store for her as a doctor's wife, she would not have been so positive in her statements about never leaving me. Every dreamy young bride whose hubby is a physician has a tough dose to swallow. She must come to realize that to all appearances her dreamboat is much more interested in the rest of the female population of the community than he is in her. And why not? He has got her for good, but Mrs. Jones might feel neglected and take her aching back to the competition. So Mrs. Jones gets the attention.

It makes no difference how green-eyed Honeybunch gets, or how often she rears up on her hind legs and paws the air,

she can expect her good dinners to spoil awaiting his arrival. When he does get home he smells so strongly of some
other woman's perfume that, unless she is a saint, she will
walk out into the kitchen, heft the meat cleaver and take
a few practice swings just in case.

Our family was always fond of Hubbard squash. Its skin
is hard and one needs a heavy cleaver or hatchet to cut it up
into baking size. I often wondered why my wife reserved this
chore for herself until I saw her attack one when she was a
bit sore about my missing a dinner party the night before.
The way she swung that hatchet convinced me that the
squash was just substituting for my noggin. Our vegetable
cellar was never again short on Hubbards.

The cause of Ruth's first and worst fit of jealousy was sixty-
five years old or more. This lady, Mrs. Napier, was a constant source of delight to me. She was the sister of a Southern
governor and the daughter of a general in Robert E. Lee's
army. To hear her tell it, she held the match to the first gun
that fired upon Fort Sumter.

She was tall and stately-looking. Even in the rocks and
desolation of Gold Hill, she never came out of the house except dressed in black silk, high-heeled shoes, and silk stockings. Around her neck she wore a long gold chain, about the
size of a log chain, from which hung a diamond-studded
locket. She looked as out of place as one of her native magno-
lia trees would have looked in a clump of the dusty stunted
junipers of the Utah desert.

When we men met her on the street it seemed natural for
us to doff our hats and do our best to make a courtly bow just
as the old colonels did in the movies we had seen of the South.
None of us, however, went so far as to grow long hair or a tiny
tuft of chin whiskers.

Mrs. Napier was in Gold Hill for one purpose only—to protect her youngest son from designing females. The stars had
ordained that of all places Gold Hill was to be her Gettys-

burg. She treated us men as if we were halfway between the old plantation servants and share croppers. Of the women she admired Daisy, the girl from over the hill, because of her tiny ankles, and she liked my wife because Ruth paid no attention to the old lady's estimate of our society and kidded the daylights out of her. Mrs. Napier had coped nicely with the Daisy Maes and Scarlett O'Haras of her own native country, but western girls were too much like the Canadian Mounties for her to understand.

When she discovered that there were no unmarried women in camp and only a fourteen-year-old girl in Ibapah and a twelve-year-old in Callao, she got careless and relaxed her vigilance.

One Saturday night there was a dance at Gold Hill which Sonny attended along with the rest of the population. A surprise awaited us when we arrived. A single girl who taught school in Salt Lake City had come out to visit her married brother. She came to the dance with Lem and his wife. All the boys made a bee-line for this treasure, but Sonny won out. Sunday morning they ran away to Salt Lake City. Monday morning they were married.

When the news reached Gold Hill we knew that Richmond had fallen again. The old lady went into the first real case of hysterics I had ever seen and topped any performance of this histrionic endeavor that I was ever to witness in the future. The girl was from a good family and seemed fitted in every way to make a good wife for a mining engineer, but mother reacted like the old parody on that song hit of the Nineties, "Sweet Marie": "Her face was pure and sweet but I faltered at her feet." The bride was a descendant of the pioneer women who walked from the Missouri River to Utah in the Mormon migration. She had muscles in her ankles instead of just tendons.

Five hundred times that day I was informed that Southern ladies all had small ankles. The rest of their shape did not

matter, but mockingbird ankles were a mark of distinction
and a necessity in good society below the Mason-Dixon Line.

I have spent forty-five years in research on this subject and
I must say that I have found just as high a proportion of "Or-
phan Annie Legs" among women who said "You-all" as
among those who said "You-uns."

I felt sorry for the old lady, as she was among strangers
who generated mighty little sympathy for her. Such queenly
old ladies were not rare in my boyhood Missouri town. Besides I was so busy cataloging a whole new set of symptoms
and filing them away in my brain for future reference that I
stayed with her almost all day.

Ruth had baked a pie and I did not get home to eat it. I
caught hell from her and then some. When she ran down we
had a little talk. She finally understood that women were my
business and that if she ever hoped to own a fur coat she
would have to depend upon demanding old ladies to buy it
for her. Peace and harmony were restored.

When the doctors in Tooele, the county seat a hundred
weary miles to the east, found out that there was a physician
out on the western desert they discovered all kinds of excuses
to avoid the long trips to care for people living closer to me
than to them. Pretty soon I was making occasional trips clear
over to Government Creek, the Simpson Springs area, and
isolated ranches seventy miles away.

In the beginning these distances seemed appalling, but
you can get used to anything. I learned to keep many spare
automobile parts in the trunk of my car along with a five-
gallon can of gasoline, a gallon of engine oil, a full water bag
and a few cans of tomatoes. The water was for the radiator.
If I got thirsty, the tomatoes relieved thirst on the desert better than any water could.

Even today no man who knows his desert ever turns off the
beaten track without assuring himself that there are a few
cans of tomatoes rattling around in the trunk of his car to

quench his thirst when the engine radiator requires the contents of the water bag.

Sometimes I ran into some queer birds on these trips. Mrs. Olsen was one of them.

The Olsens' home was the usual two-room log cabin—kitchen-living room and parlor-bedroom. The help and visitors always slept in the bunk house, a crude guest cottage present on every ranch. It was usually made of logs with a dirt roof and furnished with a big stove, some nail kegs for chairs and a row of bunks built along the wall. Everybody carried his own bedding. If the guest was a sissy, he could get a forkful of hay from the feed lot and pad the soft pine boards which served everybody else for a mattress.

When I went into the parlor to see my patient, the first thing that met my eyes was a large ornate burial casket. It sat in front of the window in the spot usually reserved for the table containing the family library—the family album, the mail-order house catalogue and the Book of Mormon. This was a bit of a shock. Upon first contact with me people had at times questioned my ability, but this was preparing for eventualities in earnest. I concluded that there was a joke-smith loose some place.

"What in hell is that thing doing here?" I inquired politely.

The old lady didn't give her husband a chance to answer. She was not too sick to talk, as is the case with most ailing females.

"No reflections intended, Doc," she said. "That casket belongs to me. About two years ago a woman died over near Gandy. They took boards off the tool shed and made a casket and covered it with cheesecloth and buried her in that. The boards had never been planed either. Last year when we were in Salt Lake City to my sister's funeral I got stuck on her casket. Before I came home I ordered one just like it. Now I can rest easy. When my time comes, I don't need to worry about splinters. See, it's lined throughout with pink satin and has my name on the top plate. Everything is there except the date of death, and Paw can file that in with a rat-tailed file when the time comes."

The last time I heard of Mrs. Olsen, several years later, she was pretty worried. She was putting on a bit of weight and confided to a neighbor that the casket was getting to be a tight fit. She went on a diet. Instead of using the bathroom scales, she would hop into that plush canoe and try it on for size.

She was not crazy. Should the end come when the roads were blocked with snow or impassable because of mud in the spring, people would have to make do with what they could get. Not everybody had a tool shed with board siding.

As I drove out to her place I went by a ranch with a nice grove of poplar trees growing about the house. The custom of the people was to halt and gossip a bit when passing any human habitation, and so I planned to stop on my return trip and get acquainted. Perhaps I would be invited to supper.

The only person at home was a tall, slender, seventy-year-old, whiskered like the Smith Brothers of cough-drop fame. He was overjoyed to see me and insisted that I stay all night.

I wasn't hard to coax. Seventy miles seems a lot longer in the dark when there is nothing to look at but the road. Besides, his kitchen looked comfortable and inviting. It was a large room that took up the entire end of a rambling log house built somewhat on the order of the modern ranch-style home. The kitchen was furnished with a big Majestic range including a big oven, a reservoir on the end for warm water, and a warming closet built high on the back. Muslin had been stretched over the inside of the log walls and a gay wallpaper pasted over it. Above the door were a couple of deer heads with the old man's rifle and worn felt hat resting upon them. In the center of the room was a big old-fashioned table half covered with magazines and bits of harness. But what warmed this weary traveler's heart was the presence of two enormous old rocking chairs generously upholstered with bed quilts. The oven door was open and the chairs so located that one could put his feet on the door and knock the ashes from his pipe into an old lard can sitting on the floor between the chairs.

Damn and double damn these modern architects who design functional kitchens that look like machine shops, and three more damns for the fiend who decided that over-stuffed chairs are more comfortable and artistic than the kind Whistler's mother occupied!

The old man hustled around and opened a can of peaches, fried some lamb steaks and made a pot of coffee. We shoved the rubbish back from one side of the table and had a feast. Afterward we occupied those rocking chairs with our pipes going nicely and the coal-oil lamp at our backs on the table.

I saw that the old man was full of talk. After assuring him that Mrs. Olsen was in no danger and relating the gossip I had heard around the desert in the last month, I settled back and let him broadcast.

His wife, he told me, had died two years before at a daughter's home in Salt Lake City. He had about quit farming. Oh, he kept a few sheep, of course, to furnish fresh meat, and a couple dozen cows running on his fenced range, his riding horse and two sheep dogs and maybe a dozen chickens for eggs in season, but the days of his active life were gone. He stated that his daughters came out a couple of times each year and cleaned up the place. He had an old car if he wanted to go visiting.

Then like all old men his mind did a flip and he was living the days of his youth over again.

"Doc," he said, "did you notice that old table we ate from? That is one reason I am staying on the ranch. I brought my bride here in a white top, camping overnight at Point-of-the-Mountain [Garfield, Utah] and at Lookout Pass in the Stansbury range. That was old Porter Rockwell's station. The third night we made a dry camp at River Bed. All our housekeeping things were packed in the wagon, and that table was tied on behind. It was a wedding present from my mother. Her dad traded a horse for it to some folks bound to California. When he got it there was some scars where arrows had struck, and there was one bullet hole clean through the center leaf.

"The poor folks had had a rough trip and quite a battle with the Indians over about Bridger's place in Wyoming. The woman cried a bit when they took the table down from the back of the wagon, but they had to have the horse.

"My grandfather knew good furniture when he saw it. He got an old walnut gunstock and made the arrow scars go clear through the wood. Then he plugged all the holes and sanded and polished the thing for weeks. He got it looking as good as new before he would let his wife use it.

"Come over here and I will show you the plugs. See those spots that are a little darker than the rest of the walnut?"

It was beautifully grained wood, and under the papers showed a high polish and smoothness.

The old man continued: "Well, sir, the house I brought my wife to was only a dugout, but we set up that table and ate our first meal in our home from it. Just the two of us and the great outdoors. Time went on and I prospered, what with sheep, teaming for the mines at Fish Springs and running a few cattle. I got enough together to build this room and we had a house to move that table into.

"Then the kids began to arrive. I tended my wife myself with every one of them. The table began to fill up, and we added more rooms to the house. When the twelfth one made his appearance I had to build an extension on the table so they could all sit down for prayers and dining. Life was pretty busy for both of us. Before we realized it the kids were flying out of the nest and I could remove the extension.

"Then the table began to shrink itself. We took out one leaf at a time. About fifteen years ago the table was back to the size it was when we started.

"Well, Mother and I had ten mighty happy years, bride and groom all over again, but no rush about anything this time; we were coming down the mountain now and wanted to enjoy each day to its fullest. We realized they were getting fewer pretty fast.

"Three years ago this month Mother got to feeling poorly and I took her in to our daughter Gracie's in Salt Lake City. She lived just a year after that. Whenever I could get to town she would quiz me about the ranch and admonish me to be careful and not do any harness riveting on her table top. Right up to the last she figured to be home soon, but she never made it.

"I've been alone now two years. I sort of hate to have the girls come out to see me. Soon as they get here they start raising hell about me living clear out here like a savage all by myself and demanding that I sell the home ranch and come and live with them. God knows, there are plenty. I could stay a month with each one and round out the year. They're not all in Salt Lake of course. Some of them live back East, and some in San Francisco, but I guess any of them could stand me a month once a year.

"I told my daughter Molly that as long as the table and I were here I felt like Mother was just away visiting, or at Conference, and would be back in a few days. But Molly said bring the table with me, she would love to have it in her drawing room—it's a genuine antique and such things are very stylish.

"Well, Doc, I know Molly. That table would stay put six months and then she would decide to have her house done over. Some morning I would find it out on the glassed-in porch, painted blue and supporting her latest bunch of African violets. The next move would be to the back porch, or her man would want some walnut to carve up on his lathe and that would be the end of our family shrine.

"They will be back next month and we will have it all to argue out again, but I'm going to shut them up the first day or else drive them off.

"I like my kids, but that table holds memories of a happy time before they ever came to make me share their mother's love. I will be damned if I'll move from this spot as long as I am able to do a little for myself.

"I've told Jimmy Olsen that if I should check in out here to be sure and use the leaves of that table in my casket and to plant me out under the poplars before he notifies the kids. I would never rest easy in such a gilded cage as his wife keeps in the front room. Here I have lived and here I intend to rest. If that table ain't buried with me, I'll sure as hell come back and haunt some of these damned smartalecky kids. Now tell me about yourself."

It was pretty late and I knew he had asked only to be polite, so I suggested that we smoke one more pipe and spend the time with our own thoughts and then go to bed.

8

Ruth Talking

My wife and I have spent many lazy summer after-
noons sitting out under the live-oak trees at our farm in Au-
burn, California, batting the conversational ball back and
forth about this chapter. I have tried to get her to write it in
her own words, but she insists that one writer in the family
is trial enough. She doubts the dog and the cat could stand
two of us. Also, like most women, she talks much faster than
she writes.

In order to make the story sound reasonable from the female standpoint I have listened to her carefully and have
filled several notebooks in order to give my readers what my
wife of forty-plus years remembers of that wonderful time
when she was a bride.

There are things in her account that do not seem reasonable to me or, I expect, to any other man. I assume no responsibility for her logic. If her reminiscences don't make sense,
don't blame me.

From here on to the end of the chapter Ruth will do the
talking.

Our honeymoon cottage was not designed for the entertainment of guests or for gracious living. I was the mistress of
an area ten feet square. There was no running water, no
kitchen sink, no built-in fixtures, no patio. Bare rocks were
the only lawn, and there was not a tree within two miles.

This little room had a stove in one corner, a kitchen cabinet in another, a sanitary cot—a folding contraption modeled after the racks in ancient dungeons—folded up against the wall, and a dressing table which took up the other end of the room. For seating we had two folding chairs and a rocking chair that had been left behind in a boxcar. We could only guess about its former history. When the cot was made up for sleeping, the chairs had to be moved into the front room or office, and, since that space was equally well occupied, piled upon the examining table.

That was the snuggest house we ever lived in. I could sit in the rocker, stoke the stove, set the dinner table and powder my face without getting up. I think the designer of roomettes in modern sleeping cars must have once lived in such a place.

For thirty years my husband has dreamed of the time when we could cut loose from all fixed living quarters, buy a trailer and see the world. I have tried to be an understanding woman. I have frozen in duck blinds, accumulated black and blue spots from sleeping on the ground while hunting, and burned myself cooking over campfires in order to be with my family of males. But if he ever gets me into one of those bouncing chicken coops he will have to give me a general anesthetic first.

I like to cook and keep house, but I do not like to have things so chummy that when I turn to the cupboard to get a pan or dish, my posterior knocks other utensils from the top of the stove. That happened many times in our Gold Hill home, and I had no middleaged spread to account for it as I weighed only a hundred and five pounds.

The thin sheet-iron stove was two feet square. It had four holes on top, a tiny oven, and a fire-box designed to contain one handful of sagebrush at a time. Such stoves were made to fit into sheepherders' wagons and were better than a campfire, but not noticeably so. The kitchen cabinet was many things in one. In the top were shelves for dishes. Below were little bins for flour and sugar and so forth. The bottom had two shelves for the cooking pots and pans. The work area pulled out far enough to make a small dining table. It was nicely finished in white enamel and there was room underneath to keep the dishpan. Because of the scarcity of water we had to save the dishwater and use it over and over again. A woman who could not make a pan of dishwater last two days was considered a wasteful housekeeper and was talked about by her neighbors.

The floor covering was a Congoleum rug we had bought in Salt Lake City on our wedding day. It was the one artistic article in the establishment. It had a blue background, and a cream-colored floral design in the middle. I kept it clean, as those were the only flowers I saw unless I got homesick and went over to Mrs. Gerster's to smell her geranium.

The first two weeks we were married I never had time to cook. After that I made my husband continue to board at the restaurant until I had made curtains of bright gingham for our one window, and for the dressing table the old miners had made for me. That dressing table was a work of art. It had lots of drawers and other handy little places to put things. It even had a trinket drawer made out of a plug tobacco box and lined with blue plush that one of the old boys had found somewhere.

I just had to have more room. Perhaps other women could keep house in such cramped quarters, but they had been married longer than I had. Besides I was anxious to try out my ability to get my own way with this new husband. The other wives' cases were hopeless as their men were wise and ignored wifely grumbles.

With Mrs. Gerster's counsel I tried out a plan. After the miners had finished my dresser I complimented them so highly that they were ready to do anything, so I dropped a hint that I would like a wardrobe to hang clothes in. Within a few days it arrived all ready for the curtains.

When my husband got home for supper he wanted to know what the hell that thing was sitting out behind the house. After I had explained its use he shook his head.

"But Ruth," he said, "if we put that thing in the house, there won't be room for us."

"Well," I said, "we just can't hurt the old men's feelings. They were so proud of it when they brought it up, I had to say it was the one thing that would make my house complete. What else could I do?"

He did not answer. The next day a man arrived and began to build the frame for a tent-house beside our back door. Pretty soon we had a twelve-by-fourteen-foot bedroom and I could truly begin to keep house. We bought a white iron bed and a big hot-blast heating stove, and lined the wood sides of the room with paper to keep the wind and snow from coming in the cracks. I have never slept in a more cozy bedroom. When there were six inches of snow on the roof of the tent and a roaring fire in the stove it was as comfortable and sweet smelling as a summer's day.

Now it was time for me to take upon myself the burdens of real housekeeping. Preparing meals, of course, was the first and most important chore. My only qualification for it was a willingness to learn. I could boil water without burning it, and was a fair chafing dish cook, but never in my life had I had a lesson in domestic science. My plan was to find out what the doctor liked to eat and then learn to cook it the way he wanted it.

It took me years, however, to learn just what he did want. He had lived in boarding houses so long that he had forgotten what he liked. He had a few peculiarities: one, he wanted no damned dried apples or peaches in the house; two, he liked hot cereal for breakfast; three, he did not like coffee;

four, he approached any new dish with all the confidence and nonchalance of a cow entering a strange barn.

I quickly mastered the technique of making breakfast mush of the Cream of Wheat, oatmeal, or plain corn meal variety. It was a good thing that I did because I have used that skill some fifteen thousand times in the last forty-odd years of our married life and will continue to do so, I suppose, as long as we two shall live. And how tired I get of it! Why were men so made that they want the same things to eat yesterday, today and tomorrow without any change whatever?

He craved home-baked bread, so I borrowed some starter from Mrs. Gerster and followed her directions. It rose beautifully but that blasted stove always burned the crust and left the middle raw. Finally I solved that problem too. There was a young married couple in Ibapah named Felt. Fay Felt and I became fast friends. Her mother-in-law had a big range, so when the day came when the doctor had to make calls in that region, I set my bread the night before. When he left I went along, with the bread riding in the car trunk. If we were delayed too long in getting to the Felts' ranch, I crawled out and pounded it down a bit. Then I baked it nicely in Mrs. Felt's oven while the doctor was calling on his patients.

The Felt family were peculiar in that they milked cows. Everyone in the valley had cattle, but everybody else used canned milk and store butter shipped from Salt Lake City. They said, and it was true, that if you wanted to milk one of the range cows you had to shoot her first and that was wasteful. I always stocked up on milk and cream when I went on a bread-baking expedition. Then when we got home I served whipped cream on everything and made myself so sick I had to take several trips to Salt Lake City to see a doctor. No doctor will treat his own wife.

Perhaps I was not so sick as I seemed to be. Those trips

meant, besides seeing the doctor, a hotel room with a bath (a true luxury after bathing in a hand basin with a quart of water), shopping in real stores, and truly eventful train trips. Before I left Salt Lake City for home at ten P.M., I could see the early picture shows. I would arrive at Wendover at two A.M. A kindly old Mexican woman who ran a rooming house on the Utah, or respectable, side of town would meet me with a lantern and take me to her house until the Deep Creek Cannon Ball was ready to start to Gold Hill. This contraption regularly ran off the track a couple of times and tossed us around a bit.

One thing I could do in my little stove was roast ducks, but a sage chicken my man brought in floored me. It was as big as a turkey. I roasted it all day, but it was so tough we couldn't stick a fork into the gravy. The next day I boiled it, and the day after we buried it. Pop has never brought in a sage hen since.

We lived mostly on smoked pork. Fresh meat we got only when some rancher killed a beef for himself and neighbors. On one such occasion I made a meat pie. My brother just had to choose that night to come to dinner. He took a piece of the crust and nailed it over the door, claiming he bent two nails before he got a hole through it. The next day I brushed it down with a broom and fed it to a burro, who seemed to enjoy it a lot.

The burros were my dispose-all. They would eat any culinary mistake and smack their lips and ask for more. In fact, they formed the habit of dropping around to my back door to wait for the next failure. If it was not forthcoming they would bray until I fixed something to shut them up. It caused remarks among my neighbors; at least I thought it did.

Only once did I see a burro bite off more than he could chew. The store delivered a sack of flour to my neighbor when she was not home. My garbage can came wandering along and spied that pretty sack. He tore it open with his teeth and ate sack and all. Pretty soon he got thirsty. He kicked the top off the neighbors' water keg and drank the contents. Then he had a belly full of paste and it did not sit well. He ran around town as if he were crazy, kicking and braying something awful. Everybody thought I had slipped him my husband's bottle of snakebite medicine. He finally digested the glue and was back again the next day as hungry as ever.

Those donkeys hated men and ran like rabbits if their master showed up, but they would follow us women all over camp. The children would get an old piece of sheet iron, wire it to a burro's tail, and all climb on the slab for a dryland sleighride. The burro would amble along as gentle as a sheep until a man approached. Then away he would break for the hills. The kids were scattered about, and the sheet iron would sail through the air behind him.

The burros belonged to prospectors. When these men arrived at a place where they hoped to stay for a while, they turned the donkeys out to shift for themselves and live the best they could until they were needed again. The donkeys ganged up and had a lovely time, and were hard to capture when needed. But once a packsaddle was on their back again, they went along as peacefully as a dog.

I loved those donkeys. Every day they covered up many more mistakes of mine than the sexton ever did for my husband. They would consume anything except a glass bottle or a tin can, were always on duty, and never broke down. And a jackass's ear is a grand place for a somewhat bewildered and homesick bride to whisper her hopes, doubts and fears. They were big, expressive ears. When I was happy, the beast would wiggle his ears in joy when I scratched them. When I was sad, he stood stock still with his ears pointed back at an angle and let me weep on his neck. He never commented upon my foolishness or violated my confidences, and was the first to hear the news when I realized that the Pecks would soon be three quarters of a bushel.

My poor husband had dreamed, I am sure, of the blissful state of matrimony as crowned by a pot of baked beans for Sunday dinner just like the ones his mother used to serve. I could not bake beans; in fact, I could not even boil them tender enough for human consumption. None of my female acquaintances could either. Hard water and high altitude just did not suit those little white bullets and we had no pressure cookers in those days. The burros ate them and I dried my tears upon their fuzzy necks. Pop had to take his beans out of a can, as he did all the other vegetables.

When the weather began to get hot in June, keeping things from spoiling became a problem. Then my old prospector friends took a hand. (I called them my Leprechauns, and Pop referred to them as the Gold Hill Sanhedrin after the time I had gone barefoot.) Anyhow, they were almost as comforting as the burros. One hot morning they came up with a contraption that looked like a rocket nose cone with a radar screen on top. It was about four feet high, roughly circular, and made out of wooden uprights. It contained three shelves, the top one about a foot in diameter and the bottom one eighteen inches. Covering the whole contrivance was burlap sacking. A door of the same material tacked to a wood frame gave access to the whole interior. On top rested a small wash basin with strips of burlap hanging down over the sides and touching the cloth below.

My friends set the thing by the back door, right in the sun, and filled the basin with water. Here, they informed me, was my desert cooler. The water soaked up into the burlap strips and ran down the sides, and evaporation did the rest.

I never had a refrigerator again that kept things as nice. Occasionally the store would get in a crate of wilted lettuce and carrots. I would buy a sackful and put them in this cooler. In a day they were as plump and crispy as the moment they were plucked from the garden. Milk would keep sweet for three or four days. Now I did not have to make a pig of myself and drink it all up in one day to keep it from going sour. There was nothing to get out of order and no electric current to pay for. All I had to do was keep the pan full of water; nature did the rest. And any kind of water would do, even what came from the Gold Hill spring, which was harder than fresh cement.

Water of any other kind was a problem. We had a couple of five-gallon pickle kegs that we took to Ibapah once a week and filled with spring water. My husband dug a hole beneath the north side of the house to store them so that the water would not boil away when the sun began bearing down. We used a rubber siphon to draw off the water.

One night somebody—of course it was I—left the cork out of the keg. A couple of days later the water began to taste funny. When I called it to my husband's attention—he was used to drinking almost anything that was wet—he said maybe I was pregnant, women in that condition often got ideas about the taste of things. I quit water and lived on cocoa made with canned milk. A couple of days later he concluded that he had a sympathetic symptom of my pregnancy. We drained the keg and found it was a field mouse that was imparting the gamey flavor. A son and heir was forgotten for the time being.

It was a real chore for me to have to use the Gold Hill water for washing. How I wished for a stream and a big smooth rock that I might wash my clothes like the women of the islands! The Gold Hill method was a science all in itself. I watched the other women do it once or twice; then we decided to try our luck. Pop constructed a little fireplace of rocks, threw an old iron grating over it and built a sagebrush fire. We filled two five-gallon gasoline cans about two-thirds full of water. When this got hot, we dumped in a can of lye.

This raised a scum of grayish bubbles clear to the top of the can, which had to be skimmed off before the soap and clothes were dumped in.

The men called this boiling process "cooking seam squirrels," but we did not harbor any lice in our house. When my husband quit bunking in the construction bunk cars he threw away all his clothes and moved into his bachelor cabin all sweet and clean.

After the garments were boiled I rubbed them on a board and dumped them into the rinse can. No matter what color they were when they went in, they came out a dirty gray. Because the burros liked them, I had to stand guard until they were dry, and forget about ironing them.

After the first washing, I saved my undergarments and stored them in a suitcase. When I went to Salt Lake City I took two suitcases, one with my clothes and one full of dirty laundry to be washed in my hotel room. We used no sheets or table cloths; gray cotton blankets on the bed got three times the mileage of white sheets before they looked soiled. Our cabinet eating-shelf was white enamel so we ate off that; when company came we used a napkin for a cloth and it went into the suitcase with my clothes. Of course, we didn't get very dirty. There was little or no dust, for there was no soil to make any. When we went to Salt Lake City we took four or five baths per day to make up for those hand-basin affairs we used between times.

Social life was almost as meager as the water. No more brides arrived, and so until the suckers came out to buy mining property we had no dances except the grand ball for the soldiers when the Indian war fizzled out. But we ladies formed a Red Cross Chapter and knit sweaters and socks in our spare time. Mrs. Gerster was always good for a cup of tea, and we visited at the Felts in Ibapah, and the Kearneys in Callao. Often we stayed at the Indian Reservation, where the agent's wife and sister made us most welcome. These ladies handled the bread situation in a way that was new to our Western eyes; they baked a big bunch of hot cakes for breakfast and ate them cold at all the other meals. My husband usually went fishing and so avoided the cold hot cakes, whenever I tried this.

Nothing serious ever happened to us but something almost did. All the coyotes were rabid, and down in the valley even the cattle, turkeys and pigs caught the disease. We were careful about going out without a gun. There had never been any rabid animals around Gold Hill, however, for we kept all the dogs muzzled.

Late one night when my husband came in tired from a trip, I discovered I was out of cocoa. (We drank gallons of the stuff; it made canned milk bearable.) I grabbed my jacket and told him I would run down to the store for some while he was getting warm. It was bright moonlight. Before I had gone five steps I saw a creature coming toward me. I could not get back into our front door as it was coming behind me, so I lit out around the tent as fast as I could go and won the race to the back door by about three feet.

"There's a coyote after me," I yelled as I burst in.

My husband grabbed his gun and stepped out. He saw an animal and blazed away. But the coyote had gone by; he killed a neighbor's dog that had been fighting with it.

Of course, the dog would have had to be killed for safety's sake. The owner was grateful because he didn't have to kill his own pet, but my husband didn't feel very heroic after that.

The men hunted that coyote all night but could not find it. Just after dawn a sheepherder up on the hill behind our house was getting his breakfast when he heard a noise behind him. Turning, he saw the coyote staggering toward him. He grabbed a frying pan full of mutton chops and beat the brute's brains out before it could harm him.

I was slightly pregnant at the time and I spent the next six months worrying about the possibilities of my baby being marked by that fright. My husband laughed at such fears, but the old ladies thought differently. When our young gentleman arrived and exercised his lungs in the middle of the night, I concluded that the old women had something that these doctors didn't know about.

It was a wonderful life. I was young and in love, with no cares and few domestic responsibilities, and secure in the knowledge that my man returned my affection. There was no need for me to worry about keeping in style in clothes, automobiles, or swimming pools. The hardships were fun, and it was a satisfaction to me that I could live and make my man happy with so few of the conveniences to which both of us had been accustomed. It was the fulfillment of a romantic dream.

How I would hate to have to repeat it!

9

Wild Horses

By June, 1917, Gold Hill began to act a bit more like a typical American community. It had grocery, dry goods, hardware and drug stores, an assay office, and a daily newspaper.

The *Gold Hill News* was not so big as the *New York Times,* nor was it so small as a postage stamp; but considering the fact that it all came in one truck—presses, paper, editor, printer, and a tent to house them—it was a pretty good paper.

The editor was not a Baron Munchausen, but he could have come in a good second in any encounter with that nobleman. If a miner set off two sticks of dynamite and knocked down three wheelbarrow loads of granite rock, the report that was heard when the *News* came out made a lot more noise. For example: "Yesterday Jno. Jones made great progress in the tunnel on the North Star and the enormous blast revealed much interesting material. Mr. Jones is now sure he will contact the real ore-bearing vein in a few days." All poor Mr. Jones had discovered was some more hard old granite, a good prospect for a tombstone factory.

The editor had run papers in all the Nevada gold camps. He knew how to spread the fertilizer to make the suckers grow.

It was he who awoke the latent missionary spirit in the rest of us. He was always sounding off about the advantages of Gold Hill as a cultural center or about how we could enrich the lives of the poor people who had been so isolated from the benefits of an enlightened society, and how it was our civic duty to bring a brighter day to the good people who lived on the ranches of the region. He did not mention the fact that those ranchers had already bought all their groceries for the next year from the United Grocery Company in Salt Lake City in one big order, and their other necessities from the mail-order houses in Chicago. They showed little interest in transferring their trade to the merchandising marts of Gold Hill.

I sometimes wonder if that editor is not still alive and active in the high places in Washington. Ever since the First World War we have been trying to uplift the small and less favored nations and create a demand for the blessings of our civilization. We have, of course, been ready to fulfill those demands at a profit.

After a few weeks of his bombardments we decided to call a Town Meeting and discuss how best we could serve these people—and move our merchandise a bit faster.

The meeting was held in the pool hall, the biggest building in town. High-minded speeches assailed our ears like a hailstorm. We should have a work day and improve the road to Callao and Trout Creek as well as fill up the badger holes in the road to Ibapah. We should send delegations of missionaries to these backward communities to win friends, and influence people to come to Gold Hill for exposure to our enlightened social atmosphere.

It was very hot that night and the pool hall was as stuffy as the Black Hole of Calcutta. Along about eleven o'clock a miner who had slept through most of the proceedings arose and made a motion that we build a road to Ferber, Nevada, another mining camp just ten miles over the mountain but forty around by the current road.

He was greeted by hoots of scorn. Ferber also had a store or two. After the chairman, the manager of the grocery, had restored order, the miner was allowed to state his reasons for such an asinine suggestion. He rose to his feet a bit unsteadily and grasping a chair for support delivered a speech which wrecked Gold Hill's high ambitions.

"Well," he said, "I was over to Ferber today and they have beer on ice."

There were yells of "Where did they get the ice?"

"They are going to get two hundred pounds of ice each day by a truck which will meet the Salt Lake train at Wendover and get it to Ferber before daylight so it won't melt on the way."

The chairman jumped to his feet and pounded his gavel until the noise quieted down. He announced that we would meet at seven o'clock at the Cain Springs mine the next Sunday morning. Everybody was to bring a pick and shovel. All the wives were to make a lot of sandwiches. A car or two would be on hand at noon to bring the women and lunch to the Ferber road builders. Then he adjourned the meeting.

Even the editor seemed pleased with this worthwhile endeavor. Nothing seemed so high-minded and culturally enlightening right then as a cold bottle with a big red "A" on the label.

The railroad construction crews loaned us a couple of rails, and mules to drag them over the ground. This gear removed the small brush and some of the rocks. We men followed to dig out the big rocks and fill up the little gullies. By noon we had reached the top of the pass. The ladies were able to travel after us without having to push the cars once.

It was a wonderful dinner. After it had been consumed, the girls joined us in throwing rocks out of the track. Before dark we had reached the banks of Deep Creek, a dry gulley twenty feet wide with steep banks fifteen feet high. There, just half a mile away, gleamed the road leading up to Ferber, three miles farther west. But we had nothing with which to tear down the banks.

We had to give up and return home. When we got there we secured some lumber from the mining company and put a carpenter to cutting out bridge timbers so that we could build a bridge the next Sunday.

Everybody was back on the job that next Sunday. First we laid a couple of six-by-six timbers over the chasm. We drove two cars over them to go forward and spy out the promised land. The Children of Israel were no more happy to see their spies return to the wilderness bearing grapes than we were to see these cars come back bearing the fruit of the hops and, oh, so deliciously cold.

During the day we got the bridge up. Everybody went on to see for himself. In the morning two cars were able to cross the gulley on six-inch planks laid parallel. Coming back, three cars missed the bridge entirely and several others insisted that the thing dodged just as they were about to drive onto it.

It was a grand project nobly conceived and masterfully executed. But how were we going to pay for the bridge timbers? Another meeting of the Boosters' Club was called. It was a pretty sober gathering until some embryonic New Dealer suggested that we invite the County Governing Board out to see it and hint that they foot the bill.

A big feast was planned, and the members of the Board were invited to visit this Western metropolis. It being an election year, they came. We detailed a couple of cars to haul them around the country and accidentally show them the new bridge, but because they were all good Mormons who never touched intoxicants unless there were rattlesnakes about and then only as a prophylactic measure, under no circumstances were they to be taken beyond that point.

The dinner that night was a huge success. If the speeches delivered there had been spread on the ground, I am sure it would have been so enriched that we could have grown flowers in the gravel. The old boys swallowed it, but one of them remarked that although he admired our initiative in building our own road and bridge instead of demanding that the county do it, still he could not see why we had gone to such an effort to build something that seemed to lead to no place in particular. However, he was happy to vote to pay our lumber bill. He only hoped that some day the reason would be revealed unto him.

Had he been in town the next weekend, he would have found out. The entire town, dogs and all, went to Ferber on a good-will tour and established most pleasant relations with the inhabitants of this desert oasis.

As in so many of our country's later good-will missions, we added a zest to our own living but neglected the poor lonesome ranchers we had set out to make happy.

Though Gold Hill's civic consciousness died a-borning, its feeble wails were heard all over the surrounding desert and stimulated the natives to similar activities. Before this time the only social affairs in Ibapah had been wedding dances and an occasional party at the school house, but that same June the inhabitants decided to hold a rodeo and invite residents of neighboring hamlets to take part therein.

The date was to be the Fourth of July. Any woman who was determined to have a baby that day would just have to do the job by herself because I intended to be at the Ibapah performance.

I had met only frustration in searching for the principal ingredient of this horse opera. There was not a ranch horse in the whole region that couldn't be ridden with a blanket for a saddle and a hackamore. When I had inquired diligently for a "bucking bronco" I was informed that such a beast was quickly sold to some sucker from the city or taken out and shot and left for the pigs to eat. When the ranchers forked Old Paint, they expected him to carry them to the place they wanted to go with as little discomfort as possible. If Paint knew his business he limited his antics to side-stepping rattlesnakes and avoiding badger holes.

The invitation to the rodeo stated that the boys were going to round up a bunch of wild ones, and there would be fun for all. A famous individual whom I shall call Bill Brown, whose reputation for sheep stealing and cattle rustling had caused him to absent himself from his native heath for some time, was back home again. Mr. Brown had made quite a name for himself in these new-fangled bucking contests which were becoming popular around the country. He was now a shining light among the cowboy actors, and had even performed in the movies as a sort of prehistoric Gary Cooper. The affair was to be under his management and the great man himself would take part.

At last I was getting close to the romance of the Old West —wild horses from the desert and wilder cowpokes from the B-bar-B in Hollywood. Many times I had seen wild horses, but because they saw me first I had had to watch them through field glasses. The magnified picture left a lot to be desired. I was sure that close up they would sport the flashing eye, the flowing mane and tail, and the unconquerable look of the monarch of the range the movies pictured.

Ruth and I set off for Ibapah early on Independence Day, 1917, full of hope and romantic anticipation. We had no trouble in securing a good seat for the festivities. The circumference of the amphitheatre, where the action was to take place, was limited only by the number of cars that could be parked in a semicircle as a barricade beyond which the horses could not run.

This exposed position made me a bit nervous. A short time before, my wife and I had been driving along a road in the hills. Above us a band of sheep were feeding. A coyote showed up over the brow of the hill, and the sheep stampeded down the grade. Some were stopped by our car; the other sheep ran right over them. Presently our little Ford was full of sheep. Even now when I describe the picture of my new bride nursing a full grown ewe in her lap and cussing me for laughing, she gets sore and swears that she wishes she had followed her inclinations at the time and gone home to mother right then.

But at the rodeo there were no fences to hide behind, so Lizzie took her place in the circle. It looked like an old-fashioned wagon train lined up to repel an attack by the savage red men.

The boss cowpoke was all that we had dreamed about, though he was garbed in raiment that was as strange as though he hailed from Mars—a bright pink silk shirt, a baby-blue handkerchief tied around his neck, and the hairiest of orange-colored chaps on his legs. His hat had a rattlesnake band, and his spurs and wide belt were apparently solid silver. He was a tall, dark and handsome specimen, with hair as black as any Indian's and as straight. In fact, he was supposed to be about a quarter-breed, but his prominent nose showed that it wasn't Gosiute blood that flowed in his veins. The Gosiutes' faces were so fat that the nose looked like a wart with a couple of dimples in it.

All the tribe had come down from the Reservation for this clambake. The Minnehahas, as well as some of their fairer sisters, sighed and breathed a bit faster when this gaily colored eagle deigned to glance in their direction. The Indian boys, got up as they were in their Montgomery Ward finery, looked pretty dingy beside this bird. However, he inspired them to do or die to attract their girls' attention, and so they rode most of the horses.

While waiting for this drama of the Old West to begin, I left Ruth to visit with her Indian lady friends and walked over to the corral to see the wild ones, or, as they are called on the desert, "pin ears." Bang went another of my romantic dreams! There were probably a half dozen of them tall enough for a man to ride without holding up his feet to keep them from dragging. Most of them had hooves so neglected that they appeared to be wearing snow shoes. They were scared stiff and huddled together in a corner of the enclosure like a flock of bewildered sheep. As a matter of fact, they looked a good deal like sheep, for the hair on their coats seemed to be growing the wrong way.

When it was time for the thing to begin, an Indian got into the corral and started the herd to running around close to the fence. Another Indian swung a rope and caught a likely beast by the neck. Then he jumped down and took a turn with the rope around a post to hold the brute until he quit fighting. Slowly the horse was dragged close to the fence. Then a coat was thrown over his head and a twitch attached to his upper lip.

A twitch is a stick about two feet long with a rope through a hole near one end. This rope is made into a loop about a foot across which the man hangs on his arm while he grabs for the horse's nose. After he gets a firm hold he slips the rope up over the soft tissues of the animal's lip and twists the stick with the other hand. Once the brute's nose is tightly constricted in this arrangement and his head covered with a coat or blanket so that he cannot see, he is a pretty tame horse.

Then he was led out into the center of the car-bounded ring, and saddled and mounted by the buckaroo. As soon as the man was safely in the saddle, off came the blanket and the twitch, and the fun began. At least, it was supposed to.

I never saw a horse buck all afternoon. Some of them lay down and tried to roll the strange thing from their backs. Some "rared up" on their hind legs and fell down, and others tried to run. That was where the automobile fence came in handy. A horse would come hell-bent for the car. About three feet from it he would plow his feet into the dirt and stop. All too often the Indian aboard did not stop with him but came sailing over his head and landed in the spectators' laps.

Everybody got bent fenders and hoods, but as these articles were made of tin and cost about two dollars for replacements, nobody cared. Besides we could straighten them with our hands well enough to serve. Who had fenders without dents anyway? The Indian riders were fat and good-natured, and nobody got hurt.

At last it came time for our modern Jehu with his gay plumage to take the spotlight and show us how it was done upon the open ranges of Hollywood. The biggest and best horse had been saved for this exhibition. When led out of the corral, he did show a bit of initiative; his blindfold slipped enough so that he could see out of one eye and he threw a front foot in the direction of the twitch bearer. As this gentleman had no desire to enter a boxing match with the animal, he dropped his twitch and ran. There was quite a bit of yelling and riding before the brute could be got back into the corral for everything to begin all over again.

Once the saddle was in place and the star mounted, everybody stood up in his car to watch the struggle.

The horse stood perfectly still for a minute and then indulged in a long drawn out yawn. The rider used his spurs and yelled, but his steed seemed to be counting the house. Finally, in desperation, he leaned far forward in the saddle and began pounding the horse over the eyes with his hat. Naturally the horse threw back its head. The cowboy's face was close, and he got the full force of the action smack on his nose.

It was a one blow battle. The rider slid down from his perch like a sack of grain, out like a light, and all his finery rolled in the dust except one orange-colored leg which stuck up like a post because his foot caught in the stirrup. The boys quickly untangled him and dragged him away like a slaughtered beef.

The horse stood like a statue while the helpers removed the gear from his back. Then he walked a few steps and began eating some hay that had been spilled on the ground earlier in the afternoon. A bit of water splashed into Mr. Brown's face and a slug of old snake bite down his throat revived him. The show was over.

I sometimes think that had *Romeo and Juliet* been performed in that country, Romeo would have been caught sliding down a pillar from Juliet's balcony minus his pants, and old man Capulet, armed with a shot gun, would have chased him through the brush. Or Little Eva would have been secretively smoking a cigar behind Uncle Tom's back as he stood looking to heaven for the chariot to carry her up among the angels. Everything in Deep Creek always went pfft.

You ask, what became of the horses? Anyone who wanted to drag one home was welcome to take his pick. The rest were turned loose to go back to their sagebrush range. And what would a rancher do with one of those things? The studs were not reliable and were shot on sight, or if young they were altered and given to the kids to train. They made the best kid ponies possible. A wild horse is not so mean by nature as some of our more favored animals. A few handfuls of chicken feed stolen from the poultry house, a little hay and grooming, and these brutes loved their masters like a stray pup. In later years I have seen a drove of them brought to Tooele for sale. In three days the streets were full of them, loaded down with from one to half a dozen kids and trotting around like so many Newfoundland dogs.

I had one experience with wild horses which could have resulted in serious injury. Thanks to the Puckish angel who looked after us desert folks, it was only low comedy.

Bill Kearney of Callao came after me one night, reporting that his sister, Mrs. Bishop of Trout Creek, was suffering from a severe and persistent nose bleed. Would I come at once?

Since my car was in the shop, I decided to ride with Bill in his brand new Saxton automobile, a delicate and fragile sort of a baby buggy to be traveling those mountain trails. The bridge was out between Callao and Trout Creek, giving us an extra forty miles to travel. Bill pounded along at twenty miles an hour across the flat desert, as the quicker I got there the less blood the lady would lose. We were within five miles of our destination when we came to dry mud lake, a circular area of about an acre of bare clay bounded by an old wash bank some ten feet high all around. We sailed up this little incline in great style.

As we started down, the headlights were suddenly full of strange shadows. In a couple of seconds we were among the shapes that made the shadows. A band of wild horses was ganged up on the lee side of this little bank, sheltered from the wind and sound asleep. We had hit the bunch dead center.

When we saw all those horses' rears looming over us, we both dived for the floor boards. For a minute the air seemed to be full of horses. When we finally crawled out of the car, which had folded up like an accordion, it seemed that the air had been full of other things too.

"I left Bill to mourn over his loss and started out on foot, wiping off manure as I went.

Luckily the Bishops had been watching for us. When they saw our lights disappear, Alf Bishop saddled a couple of horses and started down the trail to us. I met him about a mile from the wreck, climbed on one horse and set out for the ranch house at a lope.

Anterior and posterior nasal packs stopped Mrs. Bishop's hemorrhage. Then, as daylight had come, the boys and I harnessed a team and drove down to drag in the remains of that beautiful Saxton.

Legends are, I suppose, as important as facts when one is describing a country. One legend that prevailed all over the Western deserts of Utah was that of the band of ghost horses. I never met anyone who had actually seen them, but everybody knew of someone who had. They were pure white in color, larger than the general run of dull bays and spotted red-and-whites so common in the region, but try as men had for a generation nobody had ever got a rope on one or even shot one. Still it was nice to dream about a milk-white stallion standing upon some rocky point welcoming the coming sun with a neigh of defiance and the joy of being free.

Since promising in the preface of this book that I would stick within a reasonable distance of the truth, I have regretted my action. It would be fun to write about how the hero saved the ranch for Little Nell by capturing that monarch of the wilderness and selling him for a polo pony. Maybe it is better this way, though; we can all make up our own romances as suits our fancy.

I have been trying to keep medicine out of this story also. The reader will find no pages devoted to my heroism in battling the Grim Reaper, or breathtaking tales of my saving Little Nell's life by some skillful operation on a kitchen table. I have seen some of those kitchen table productions; though the doctor usually got praise for his bravery, the patient usually died. But my professional duties do seem to creep in under the tent flaps at intervals.

When some ranch hands were rounding up a bunch of pin ears to drive into the settlements, the mount of one of the riders stepped into a badger hole and caused a bad spill. The man seemed seriously hurt. I was called to do what I could for him.

I arrived about midnight and found him delirious from a high fever. The men said he had lit on his head upon the frozen ground. I thought perhaps there had been some brain injury; that sometimes causes a rise in body temperature. In that country one had to make a diagnosis and give a prognosis on the spot. But the only light available was a lantern, and so I decided to stay until morning to have a better look at my patient.

The bunkhouse was full. The only vacancy was in the patient's bed, so in I crawled beside him. I was not in the habit of going to bed with my patients, but the place was cold and a feverish bedfellow made sense to me at the time. I slept pretty well.

The next morning when I examined my bedfellow, I found him broken out with smallpox. I made a few remarks upon the subject, and before I knew it I was alone with my patient. That gang of men scattered like a flock of quail. It took me two weeks to run them all down and vaccinate them.

Once when a lady patient was having a baby, things seemed to be moving so slowly that the midwife suggested I lie down on the other side of the mother's big double bed and take a nap. I was pretty well worn out from lack of sleep. She said she would call me when I was needed. I went sound asleep. When I awoke, everything was as quiet and peaceful as a May morning. The new baby was in his crib, and everyone else was asleep. I learned that things had gone along all right and that the mother had begged the nurse not to awaken me as I seemed so tired. I was handy if needed, she said. The nurse had delivered the baby. All I contributed to the affair was a few snores as background music.

That nap cost me twenty-five dollars, as I didn't have the courage to charge a fee. I felt lucky enough that they didn't bill me for lodgings.

Not everyone was as lucky in encounters with wild horses as Bill Kearney and I were. One fellow who wasn't so lucky said that his name was Jack Smith and that he was an experienced ranch hand and a first class horse rider. This last statement proved false, so we must doubt the truthfulness of the first.

He walked into the Anderson ranch yard one June morning looking for work. His story was that he had been robbed of his car by some hitchhikers who turned him out on the desert to shift as best he could while they drove off along the Lincoln Highway with the stolen property.

It was a busy time on the ranch, and the Andersons were glad to find help knocking at the door, particularly such an accomplished individual as this one claimed to be. Mr. Anderson, however, became suspicious of his new employee's story the very first evening, when he asked the man to go milk the cows. Much to his astonishment the newcomer took the milk pail and set off for the barn without a murmur. He milked the old bossies too. That was a switch. No self-respecting cow hand would acknowledge proficiency in this menial chore. That was supposed to be the duty of old men, women, and calves. He would have promptly saddled up and ridden off if the ranch manager had even suggested that he so degrade his profession. But this man was strong and willing with a pitch fork and post-hole digger, and was put down as a brand-new breed of cow-poke. The female help were strongly in favor of the innovation.

Things went along nicely. The men discounted Jack's stories about his proficiency in all ranch activities, but he seemed to do well enough with the chores assigned him. Although he was loud in his praise of his own abilities, he was vague about his past life, offering no identifying data except that he had learned cow-poking on a big spread in Texas.

Then came Sunday. Regular work was taboo among these

good Mormons, but church was fifty miles away and after morning prayers the day would have been an awful bore unless the hands were allowed a bit of relaxation. What could be more relaxing after a hard week in the saddle than breaking some new riding ponies?

There was one youngster in the corral that gave promise of some real sport. He had been raised a pet, but for one reason or another his education had been neglected until he was a well-developed horse, big, strong and full of the devilish tricks the men had taught him during his adolescence. After dinner this animal was taken out into a plowed spot where he would be hampered in his antics by soft footing. Should the rider be unhorsed, he would have nice soft dirt to land upon. He was saddled without difficulty. One of the regular hands mounted and kept the brute's head up by tight reins. Except for some efforts on the part of the horse to bite his rider's legs, and a few crow-hops, the ride was uneventful.

Jack was somewhat scornful of the precautions. He insisted that he be allowed to mount the animal, for he was sure he could show some fancy bucking and bronc-riding. Against his better judgment Mr. Anderson allowed him to try it. Once in the saddle, Jack gave the horse his head. The brute broke for the fence, bucking and kicking high in the air. Just as the animal crashed through the fence, the rider took off like a sputnik whose apogee was a good ten feet. Instead of falling relaxed as a good rider or football player is taught to do, Jack came down all sprawled out, and landed on the back of his neck on the rocky ground beyond the fence.

The men, unlearned in the technique of handling such accident cases, carried him into the bunkhouse like a sack of flour, adding further injury to the already serious situation. The Doc was sent for. When I arrived several hours later, Jack had gone from this world. His cervical vertebrae had been crushed.

A search of his bed roll showed nothing to identify him except one page of a letter, written evidently by his mother, in which she prayed that he had learned his lesson and would now be a good boy and come home. Unfortunately it was one of the middle pages. There was no signature or address. So we had no idea just who he was or where he came from, a common situation on the desert. In contrast to the small settlements of the East and Middlewest, it just wasn't polite out there to inquire too closely as to a man's past life unless there was reason to suspect his proffered statements; then the sheriff did the investigating. Our sheriff did his best to notify all the law officers in Texas of the accident, but received no answers. So it was decided to bury the poor chap as an unknown Jack Smith.

It was against the nature or teachings of the Mormons to lay anybody away without proper religious rites. Since no one knew the religious convictions, if any, of this deceased it was decided to give him a regulation church funeral.

I had heard about Mormon funerals from other Gentiles, who were not inhibited about authentic statements, and so made a trip to the little country meeting house to attend this one. We doctors are not in the habit of attending funerals. If the late lamented is some other doctor's patient, it might seem that we are enjoying the proceedings too much; and if the party is one of our own patients, we avoid the ceremonies because of a sort of a guilty feeling. At least we imagine the rest of the audience are looking at us and thinking, "There goes the cause of it all."

But this boy was dead before I arrived, and I saw a chance to investigate the stories I had heard. I went to smile, but I came away with a greater feeling of brotherly love than I had ever experienced.

A Mormon funeral is in no way comparable to the cut and dried rituals performed by most sects. The atmosphere is not one of extreme sadness or the hopelessness of the unbelieving, but more of an enactment of that little quotation, "Say not 'Good night,' but in some brighter clime, bid me 'Good morning.'" They believe so implicitly in the resurrection of the individual and his finding his family unit established and awaiting his arrival, that their farewells are more on the order of *au revoir* and *bon voyage*. The group of people gathered to consign a friend to his Maker are merely parting from one they confidently expect to see again looking pretty much as he did when they last saw him in health. They are sure the reunion will be a happy one.

What a curse medicine is to its disciples, making so many of us non-believers!

There are usually two or three speakers at a Mormon funeral, and it lasts close to two hours. The first speaker acts somewhat like a judge and lays down the divine law as interpreted by the Mormon faith. The second speaker presents the case for the defense. Sometimes he has to rake his brain for nice things to say about the life of the deceased, and sometimes he indulges in a bit of embroidery on the facts. This custom gave rise to the tale of the widow who insisted that the casket be opened before it was removed from the church; from the description she doubted it was her late husband they had been talking about.

Since there was little known about Jack Smith, this speaker stressed his willingness to assume the duties of milkmaid because he was so grateful for the kindness of the ladies at the ranch, and what a willing worker he had proved himself to be. The third speaker talked upon a more earthly plane and warned the youth of the congregation about the folly of young men wandering off from the family fireside with nothing upon their person to identify them.

There were fervent and heartfelt prayers offered for the parents of the young man, that they might somehow learn he had been laid away by sympathetic friends and was now at peace, his race run, his story finished. The congregation sang a hymn, and then we went to the cemetery. The grave was dedicated to God by the local Church Leader, and the body was laid away with as much tenderness as if he had been the President. Once the gravel and sand had been rounded over the burial spot, the children of the congregation decorated it with sego lilies, Indian paint brush, and other desert flowers. A board was erected bearing the name Jack Smith, age and place of birth unknown. So they left him, having fulfilled the admonition of the Golden Rule.

Thus ended the life saga of Jack Smith in a little desert cemetery in one of the valleys of the Utah mountains—a human being born, grown to manhood, and gathered to his Maker. All we ever knew about him was that he could milk a cow but could not ride a wild horse.

On one of my long, late trips I came up against another facet of the universal man that a desert doctor was supposed to be. When I arrived at an isolated little cabin I found a ten-months-old boy about to succumb to a virulent attack of scarlet fever.

I could hardly believe my eyes. Three older children in the family showed the desquamation that almost always follows this disease. They gave a history of being in Salt Lake City visiting grandma a couple of weeks before. Upon their return they suffered from a slight sore throat. The poor baby had been the recipient of these imported streptococci.

In those days we had no antibiotics or any other defense against this killer except good nursing and prayer. I decided to stay all night and see the mother through the worst of the catastrophe. As was common then, the father and the rest of the family moved out as soon as I had diagnosed the case, and went to live in the bunkhouse. Everyone was properly afraid of this type of infection, and my assurances that the other children had recovered did nothing to quell their fears.

The babe passed away about daylight. Soon afterward I started to drive home.

I had reached home and had got about five hours' sleep when the father drove up to my house in Gold Hill. His neighbors had gathered and decided that the funeral must be held out of doors. No one should enter the house until some vile smelling candles had been burned therein, and the mother should not associate with the rest of the family until all this had been done and she had time to get rid of her own germs. Why they thought a doctor could associate with the sick and go about the neighborhood without scattering the same germs, I will never know. People were not so enlightened on health matters in those days. I suppose they believed the doc had some kind of personal fumigation process all his own that made him immune to every type of infection.

The man had got a casket and shoved it in through the window to his wife. She had dressed her babe for burial, but at the last moment she could not bring herself to lay the little chap into his burial case. Would I make a return trip and perform this last service for the little one? I would comfort his wife by relieving her of the task and being with her at the time of the open air services, which she could watch only through the window.

I guess I growled a bit about the superstitions of the human family, both white and red. I had more patience with the Indian's credulity than with that of the white man, but I was learning that we are all brothers under the skin. I had better accept such beliefs than "kick against the pricks" and engage in long and useless arguments.

Back I went and for a second time in my life took over the services usually rendered by the undertaker. I have always been happy that I insisted that the mother's gratitude was payment enough for such services. As the Lord told Peter, "Lovest thou me? Feed my sheep."

I did not try to qualify as a shepherd of souls, but sometimes this scattered band of sheep needed more than ministering to their aches and pains. Eventually I was to learn that a doctor must play many parts ranging from father, priest, medical adviser, friend in need, even at times savior of broken romances, as well as undertaker. It seemed that I had more things to do than a drummer in a band. If I struck a false beat now and then, I was always forgiven by my clientele.

--◆{ 10 }◆--

Robber Barons
and Swindlers

The Lincoln Highway, now designated as Highway 50, was the first effort at a coast-to-coast route for motorists. Instead of joining Highway 40 at Salt Lake City, as it does now, and using the same road as far as Wendover, Utah, where it turns south to Ely, Nevada, it was routed south from Salt Lake City through Tooele and Rush valleys. It joined the old Overland Trail at the foot of Look-out Pass through the south end of the Stansbury range of desert mountains.

Once over this range, the road led westward over a sagebrush desert for about thirty miles to Dug-way Mountain. This flat was designated as Skull Valley. Today it is the center of an enormous testing range for the U. S. Army. Where once there was nothing but coyotes and wild horses, now there are golf clubs, P.T.A.'s and other blessings of civilization, all made possible by an underground water supply over which passed hordes of thirsty men for a hundred years before someone thought to bore a well there.

Once over Dug-way, the road crept down into the Fish Springs Valley. It detoured around the brackish swamps there, then after about twenty miles of almost impassable road arrived at Fish Springs Station, a spot made famous by Mark Twain in *Roughing It*. Here was the only water between Simpson Springs at the beginning of the desert and Callao Valley, which was fed by the streams of Mt. Ibapah. That was a distance of over a hundred miles, long

138

dusty miles with nothing to see but stunted sagebrush and shad scale bushes.

Fish Springs Valley was the undisputed kingdom of John Thomas, who owned all the water. He was a man whose appearance and demeanor were the counterpart of the story book descriptions of what a king should look like. He was six feet four inches tall and four feet wide, and he had a voice that could be heard clear across the valley. It took a generous supply of rocket fuel to start him in the morning, but once he got going he was a dynamo of energy and good humor. He was a rough old diamond, and the country he lived in was not likely ever to smooth him up. A member of a breed of Americans as rare now as the dinosaur, he conformed to nothing but his own desires. He was absolute monarch of an area as large as some European states, with a resident population of two: Charley, his only subject and close friend, and himself.

King John was not bothered by neighbors, and his cattle never strayed far from home. In fact, the principal duty of his cowboy consisted of sitting on top of the bunkhouse with a pair of field glasses, looking over the area for some foolish cow that had ventured too far out into the swamp and got stuck in the mud. Should one be spotted in this situation, Charley rode out with a rope, threw a loop over the cow's horns and with the lariat tied to his saddle horn got the pony to pull her out.

King John prospered mightily from the conviction, seated deep in the mind of every man behind an automobile wheel, that signs are to be ignored.

About three miles east of his ranch house the road approached the south edge of the swamp. Here it divided. A large sign stood in the middle of the fork, to warn travelers to take the hill road in case of rain. Some frustrated tourist who had a can of paint in his trunk had added, "In case of rain go back home."

The lower road, which was ten miles shorter, skirted the swamp on pretty firm ground for a mile. Then there was another sign which read, "Stay in the road, the shoulders are dangerous." Any red-blooded American would naturally retort to this, "The hell you say," and use his own judgment.

This was all made land. That is, the rushes had grown and died over the centuries, and in spots had made the surface strong enough to support a car. Even so, if you threw a rock down on the ground you could feel the shock wave and see the earth tremble beneath your feet. The road across this neck of land was so rough and full of ruts that the surface of the surrounding area seemed smooth and inviting. It was solid enough when one walked out upon it, and it looked like a race track compared to the traveled highway. The distance was only a half mile across. Why shouldn't one pull out upon this smooth surface and show the sign makers up? The car would go fine for the first ten feet. Then plop, she would sink to the running boards with a sickening gurgle.

Close inspection now revealed another sign a hundred yards ahead. It read, "If in need of tow, light fire." A little mound of dry sagebrush was kept piled at the foot of it.

The first whiff of smoke brought old John riding a saddle pony and leading two powerful draft animals that had been standing harnessed in the barn all day ready for just such an emergency. John also brought a reel of measuring tape along. The first thing he did was measure the distance from the front wheels of the marooned car back to the rutty road. Then he announced that the fee would be one dollar a foot to drag the car back to firm ground.

He would let the driver argue five minutes. Then he raised the price to two dollars a foot, and in ten minutes to three. There was no compromise, take it or stay there.

Sooner or later the driver realized that by calling John a robber he was getting nowhere fast. He would pay the bill, and the horses would drag him back to firm ground in a hurry.

John would look over the party of travelers before they got started again. If they had kids and seemed to be in tight circumstances, he was likely to refund the entire fee, give them a long lecture on obeying the highway signs, and wave them on their way. But most of the people who traveled that road were well able to pay. They were looking for adventure and finding it.

Once the car was on the firm ground, the mud oozed in and filled the holes the wheels had made. A few hours of hot sun obliterated the tracks and set the trap for the next victim. A hundred dollars a day during the summer was a pretty good sideline for a rancher when cows sold for three dollars per head.

John was called by a good many names, none of them complimentary. Robber Baron or Robin Hood were as appropriate as any of them. He stuck the rich and helped the poor and unfortunate, but his dignity more nearly resembled Friar Tuck. I spent many happy hours listening to the tales of the great and near great in that old stage station, and had the sad experience of sitting at his bedside when this rugged individualist breathed his last. I have checked with his only living close relative, a daughter, and she has given me permission to repeat some of the stories about him, stories which are absolutely true.

One concerns the great Eddie Rickenbacker, who was driving east in some kind of modified racing car, trying for a record over the new Lincoln Highway. He stopped at Callao, filled up with gas and oil and sailed by Fish Springs Station without even a wave of the hand. In half an hour he was back there, but this time on foot. He was looking for a pull out of the mud.

John and his man Friday, old Charley, went out with the team and pulled him back on the road. John stated his fee.

The big Rick exploded and refused to pay so much for so little.

John just waved his hand, and Charley hooked the team to the front of the car and pulled it back into the deep mud again.

This about drove the great man crazy. He peeled a saw-buck from his well padded roll and yelled, "Get me out of there. I have a schedule to keep up. We are just wasting time."

"Now just a minute," John replied. "We pulled you ten feet back into the road and ten feet back out to your original position. It will take ten feet of pulling to get you back on the road again. That will be three times ten which is thirty dollars. Pay up before we move you a foot."

Eddie paid. He climbed into the car, pulled down his goggles, and tried the engine. Then he leaned out and called John many things worse than Robber Baron.

Another time a rich old lady was driving west with her chauffeur and her maid in one of those 1917 Packards that looked like a street car. When John arrived to help them she was spouting off like Old Faithful and blaming the mud on poor old John. The old lady got out of the car the better to impress John with her importance. She sank down in the muck clear to her silken covered ankles.

John yelled, "Lady, get out of that mud, it's dangerous." He pointed to some posts sticking up about two feet out of the mud. They had been put there to guide travelers upon the safe but rutty road. "See that little post beside you? Last week the telephone company placed that there. It was twenty feet high then. It has sunk into the mire eighteen feet in six days."

She got out in a hurry and was silent until they reached the ranch house. Then she stated that she had decided to eat her lunch here but would like to see the cook who prepared the meals.

"Sure," John said, "that is Charley. He will get dinner as soon as he finishes feeding the pigs."

Once again the old lady called her underlings and got ready to travel, vowing that she would never think of eating in such uncouth surroundings. When they were ready to depart, she inquired, "My good man, how far is it to the next settlement where we can get a decent meal?"

John forgot Callao and replied, "Ibapah Station. One hundred miles over the next range of mountains."

There was a consultation in the car, and then she climbed out. "On second thought," she announced, "we will dine here."

"No, you won't," John said. "We have the same cook we had ten minutes ago. Beat it out of here before I sic the dogs onto you."

Poor old girl, every wish obeyed without question in New York and refused a crust of bread in Fish Springs! She missed something. Charley was some cook, particularly with wild Mallard duck. And with good reason: the supply was unlimited.

This knack of Charley's caused John some momentary embarrassment one evening when he went out to rescue a car and found it contained the Governor of the state and one of his staff.

It was late when they got clear, and His Excellency decided to stay the night and drive on early next morning.

John was somewhat excited with the visit of a neighboring monarch and told Charley to fix up a good dinner. In the meantime he brought out a couple of bottles of Old Crow to help while away the time.

Pretty soon they heard a shotgun blasting out in back of the house. John remarked that the coyotes were pretty bad and Charley was scaring them away from the poultry run.

When they were all pretty well oiled, they sat down to

dinner. The Governor commented upon the beautiful roast duck. Out of season too!

John replied: "Why, Governor, those are tame ducks. We have a flock of them out in the chicken house. We never break the game laws or any other kind except we keep a little whisky around for snake bite." (Utah was dry in those days, and between them they had just disposed of a quart of Old Crow.)

Things went along pretty comfortably and John was beginning to breathe easier again when the Governor spit out three or four number six shot and looked inquiringly at his host. John had to think fast.

"You know, Governor," he said, "we have a curious weed in this country that the ducks are plum crazy about. The seeds look and feel exactly like bird shot. You should take some home and plant them in the waters of your duck club."

The old man smiled and turned to his aide.

"Go out to the car and get a quart of that snake bite medicine that the Governor of Nevada just gave us. It is manufactured in Scotland, Brother Thomas, and recommended highly both as a remedy for rattlesnake bites and as a powerful digestant. I am sure the stuff will digest these peculiar seeds."

John told me that it tasted like a backhouse on fire, but it sure did have the authority. Before going to bed he had promised the Governor to vote the Democratic ticket in the next election. He was certain no brew made with human hands could so upset his judgment as to desert his beloved Republican Party. He avoided that Scottish mist forever after.

Watching Charley pull a cow out of the mud got me into an awkward situation some time later and proved again that a little learning is a dangerous thing. Another city slicker and I were at Salt Springs one night, sleeping in an old sheep camp in order to be on hand for the morning flight of mallards. Long before daylight we were awakened by the bawling of a cow critter close by. As soon as it got light enough to see, we investigated and found a yearling steer caught in a sink hole and frantic with fear. He had stepped upon some rushes which gave way under his weight, and now he was half under water. Only his front legs were hanging on the solid ground of the path. In these swamps there was no bank for an animal to catch his rear feet on; even the bird dogs had to be helped out of the water when they went to retrieve ducks.

As I had seen old Charley perform such rescues with ease, I suggested to my companion that we observe Be-Kind-to-Animals-Week and snake the thing out of there. I had a half-inch manila rope in the car which I used for towing purposes when I found another car stuck, or tied on my own front axle if I was the unlucky one. I made a slip knot in it and proceeded to throw my twine over that critter's head. I could have easily stooped over and adjusted the rope, but I wanted to do it in cowboy style.

During the confusion of casting it the rope got pretty wet, but I finally had it snugly settled about the animal's head just behind the horns. My friend reached down into the water and grabbed the brute's tail. I pulled and he lifted, and finally we got the animal up enough so that a rear foot caught in the rushes. Out of there he came with a rush and made right for me.

I went up into the sheep wagon in nothing flat. My companion sneaked around on the other side and climbed in too. There we were besieged by a five hundred pound steer with horns a foot long and pretty sharp. His subsequent actions made us decide that we had roped a rabid critter, for instead of wandering off and eating grass he just walked around that wagon bellowing and rubbing his head on the ground.

We tried to send the dog after him, but the dog was an English setter and refused to work on anything but feathered game. So we had to sit cursing the steer and our own good intentions while the ducks sailed all around us just beyond shotgun range. We sat there for two hours.

Finally the brute wandered off still bellowing and rubbing his head and trailing my tow rope. For forty years I wondered what made that brute so mad. Once I was retired and a small time farmer I learned that a tight rope around the base of a critter's horns gives that animal a man-sized headache. Charley's rope was made of smooth material and the slip knot was constructed so that as soon as the pull was relaxed it slipped loose and was easily recovered. Besides, Charley was on a horse. These wild cows were used to men on horseback, whereas a man on foot looked to them like a coyote or a wolf. It was something to be charged and driven away from the herd.

How long that wet old rope constricted the circulation in the steer's head I do not know. I did not bother to ask. I knew that I was a greenhorn and I did not care to be kidded about my kindly impulses. Besides the rope might get caught on a bush and the animal starve to death. Then the owner might demand that I pay for the critter. Since that unfortunate occurrence I have restrained myself when the opportunity arose to help a strange critter in distress.

We didn't get any ducks.

By this time I had the opportunity to absorb a bit of geology and mining without recourse to books. Like an inquisitive puppy sniffing around a gopher hole, I began to spend my spare time around the Gold Hill prospects and to latch on to every visiting geologist I could meet.

One chap about my own age spent a couple of weeks

going over the country. We crawled into every hole we could find, and he hammered around and picked up specimens for study. On the last day before his return to New York, where he was to report to his company, we climbed to the top of Clifton Mountain. After he had sketched a bit he folded up his book and gave me the lowdown on the region.

"Now Doc," he said, "it is like this. The Clifton range is a very old mountain and was once much higher than it is now. The sedimentary rocks—those that settled last and were on top—have all eroded away and the mineral values with them. You will find all that down in the old lake bed. All we have here is granite. The ore bodies that seem so promising on the surface are what was left when the erosion was slowed down. None of them will go down over fifty feet in depth. Most of these prospects can mine about a ton of copper ore from the grass roots and then fold up. But that does not mean the camp will not flourish for about a year. There are a lot of slick characters mining the safety boxes of the greedy suckers back east right now. Until their pasture dries up you will find Gold Hill doing all right for itself. I am not advertising my findings around the town, but my company will not sink one dime in it."

I was not too surprised or disappointed at what he said, though I did not take the trouble to check his conclusions with any others of the profession. I expected to be in the Army before the end he prophesied, and I had already reaped my reward from the construction company. I was just killing time there until my call came from Uncle Sam.

I felt pretty sorry for some of the people who were so sure they had an eldorado this time, but disappointment means nothing to a miner. He is always going to hit it next time. They were gamblers anyhow, just playing on the dry and rocky hills instead of on the green covered tables. They were as powerless to quit as the suckers that came to Nevada after them and tried to break the bank at Las Vegas.

All this bad news did not keep me from doing a little prospecting on my own. "Rockhunting" it is now called. I had seen a beautiful specimen of tourmaline from the east side of Clifton Mountain. It was as clear and as blue as a summer sky, and I wanted some that I could have made into cuff-links.

Ruth accompanied me on my excursions, but only as far as the nearest juniper. There she would sit in what shade was available and play with chipmunks. As a child she had learned to make some sort of squeaky little call that brought all the beggars running. As she usually had a bag of pine nuts in her pocket, by the time I got back from my search there would be two or three sitting gravely on her lap cracking nuts and having a banquet.

I finally found the right specimen, but before that I had a short but severe attack of prospector's insanity. On one of my trips I picked up a piece of dark blue rock which was rather light in weight but beautiful. Every way I turned it copper tints would manifest themselves in a new flash. This was surely float. By searching the mountain above it I might just find the ore body from which it had been washed.

I was pretty smart by this time and could tell quartz from granite almost at once. Now I thought I had found a rock that must be pure copper. The ore looked as copper ought to look and must be a lot richer than the dirty green and yellow stuff the other miners went nuts about. I knew tha pyrites of iron looked more like gold than gold did, but surely nothing could outshine this real copper I had.

Like all good miners I kept still about my find because I did not want a stampede of prospectors helping me with my search. I spent all my spare time the next week crawling around that rocky hillside in the hot sun. Luck was with me. I finally found some more of the ore just sticking out of the ground. Now I had it made!

I measured off my claim and built rock monuments at

each corner and a large one in the middle. In that I placed
an empty tobacco can with a description of the claim and
my ownership by right of discovery. Then I rushed back
to camp and exhibited my findings to the first old miner I
met.

He did not seem very excited. "Yes, Doc," he said, "that
sure is pretty. Why don't you dig out a nice chunk and have
it polished and use it as a door stop in your office?"

Door stop, my eye! I intended to take it to Salt Lake City
and sell my claim for a million dollars.

"Nope," he replied. "That is copper ore all right, peacock
copper at that. But it ain't worth ten cents a ton at the smel-
ters. There is just enough copper in it to make it look pretty."

Nevertheless I carried my specimen around in my pocket
like a real hard-rocker and showed it to every sucker I
thought would not know its real worth.

A man showed up in town one morning dressed in true
storybook fashion as a real he-man of the West. His plumage
was about what I had assumed when I first set out for the
desert—high-topped boots, flannel shirt, fancy pants and
all. Here was a real sucker. I quickly struck up an acquaintance with him and showed him my specimen.

He got out his magnifying glass, licked the rock and then
examined it carefully. Finally he handed it back and offered
me five dollars for my claim. He did not ask its value and I
felt five dollars was a fair price so we made a deal. Thereupon I went out of the mining business.

A couple of weeks later the camp was thrown into a fit
by the *Gold Hill News* report of the sucker's purchase of
Ophir mine for several thousand dollars. Everybody gained
a new respect for the seller of this amateur rock quarry,
and fell over themselves begging him to tell them how he did
it. But he clammed up and left town before we learned his
secret.

This episode brought new hope to the "diggin's." The

folks who were about to move away decided to stick around
a bit and see what happened.

We did not have long to wait. Within a fortnight a carload of machinery arrived. Some workmen came out and in-
stalled an air compressor and a hoisting engine on the property, ran them for five minutes and left. Most of the oldsters
had seen such traps set before but were puzzled as to where
the bait was coming from. There was not enough good ore in
the camp to bait a mouse trap, to say nothing of this
elaborate layout.

Being an innocent in this badger game, I was somewhat
surprised when an old miner came to me one day and
wanted to know the location of the claim I had sold to the
Eastern big shot. He claimed he was supposed to do some
assessment work upon it. I told him.

A few days later I was astonished to see a wagon loaded
with my beautiful peacock copper being hauled through
town in the direction of the Ophir. About a week later old
Fancy Pants himself arrived and offered high prices for
every car in the region for one day's work. There was, he
said, a trainload of investors coming out from Pittsburgh to
look over the mining properties of the district. We were supposed to transport them to the mines and back. When the
train arrived there were about a dozen of us parked by the
depot. What a treasure for an old car collector!

There was a Hupmobile with a radiator spout a foot high
and a thermometer mounted on top of that; a Saxton; a
couple of Buicks that you started by inserting the crank just
in front of the rear wheel as though you intended to milk it;
a couple of Quad trucks that were supposed to have a power
unit on each of their four wheels; and a lot of Fords with
brass radiator housings and two-inch spouts on top for pour-
ing in mush and anything else recommended to stop the
leaks therein. But outshining us all was a brand new Scripps-
Booth belonging to a transcontinental tourist. It had broken

its axle within the first five hundred miles and now sported a handmade one that a local blacksmith had converted from an old rake tooth.

The boss man assigned this gay equipage to some portly old gentlemen who looked like money and smelled like money. Unfortunately they had to walk the last mile, as the Scripps-Booth did not have the power to climb the hill. Before we started he called all of us drivers together and told the rest to take it easy and allow the visitors to view the scenery. He would ride with me and go on ahead.

The Hup driver, an old timer, inquired, "What scenery?"

The boss brushed off his sarcasm. "Oh, just anything. These birds have never been on the west bank of the Mississippi River before. It's all scenery."

We started. He directed me to pour on the coal and we reached the top of the hill about ten minutes before the other cars showed up. He had me stop there where he could see both the mine down in the canyon and the road back down the other side of the hogback where the cars would appear.

It was as silent as a graveyard. I could see a few men sitting around the tunnel mouth and all looking our way. When the cavalcade appeared from the direction of Gold Hill my companion turned toward the mine, waved his hat and climbed back into the car. Suddenly the stillness was shattered with the boom of the exhaust from the compressor. Everybody at the mine seemed to be running around like crazy ants. As we led the procession down to the tunnel face I was somewhat astonished to see a skip full of my peacock copper ore come sailing up out of the hole and dumped near the entrance. (A skip is a little mine car holding about a wheelbarrow load of rock.)

I guess my eyes were a bit more popped than usual because another driver walked up to me and said in a low voice, "What's the matter, Doc, didn't you ever play skin the cat when you were a boy?"

I hung around long enough to get a peek into the tunnel. When I saw little chips of my peacock ore tastefully stuck into the cracks and seams of the granite wall, my Methodist-trained conscience took over and I got the hell out of there.

A big dance for the visitors had been arranged at which we local folks were supposed to appear in Western costumes. A carload of Indians from the reservation were imported to give color to the occasion. I had the only six-gun in town, a skimpy little Colt .32, but I did not get to wear it. A friend took over the honor and went outside at proper intervals to bang away at the neighborhood stove pipe chimneys and enliven the party.

In the meantime I had compromised with my conscience. I would not blow the whole thing unless someone asked my advice. I thought it best to stay away from the party as I would have to answer truthfully should a stranger request my opinion.

I could have saved myself the struggle. Inquiry after the suckers had left disclosed that not one of them ever mentioned the mines to a local citizen. They were full of the wonders of the country and what a nice man the promoter was. But they evidently placed no value upon local opinion of the investment.

This skin game was repeated two or three times that summer, but always upon suckers from a new fishing hole. We never saw another gang from Pittsburgh. They were all alike in regarding the local inhabitants as half-wild savages and not likely to advise them properly for fear they would reap all the benefits and so rob us of a good thing.

One local wag swore that he had been approached by a New York investor and that he had outlied the promoter upon the beauties of the prospect. He stated that the New Yorker had the same name and looked just like the s.o.b. who had sold him an interest in the Brooklyn Bridge during his one and only visit to the big town.

Our people were well paid for the use of their cars, and refreshments were free at the dances but, unless it was the Indians, nobody got a cent for the whooping, tooting, shooting reception we were supposed to provide as entertainment. The native ranchers were all of Mormon stock and took no part in these high jinks, but the mining population mostly hailed from Nevada.

That state was predestined to be the great equalizer. The gold bricks we westerners purchased in Wall Street returned with interest when the brokers tried to buck our samples of sound investments. Both of us could have avoided the mistakes by investigation of the property, but money was kept in circulation.

Who knows, perhaps there is still ore in the Clifton mountains. Long shots have won races, and slot machines sometimes pay jackpots.

11

Missionary to the
Gosiutes

My association with the Gosiutes began in March, 1917. It somewhat resembled the arrival of the Connecticut Yankee at the court of King Arthur, except that the Merlin I met had a few tricks up his sleeve that Mark Twain left out of his story in order to make it come out right.

I was a horrible example of the smug middle-class culture of the period, not to mention a lot of other drawbacks I possessed. First, I was of Virginia stock and had been raised to believe that people who hailed from any place else were unfortunate and to be pitied. Second, I was a Methodist. I was convinced that all non-believers who danced and played cards were on a fast train to hell. Third, I was born and bred a Democrat and believed all Republicans were "malefactors of great wealth" and to be shunned. Lastly I had spent four years sitting at the feet of teacher-physicians who believed that an M.D. after your name denotes omnipotence. To them Mrs. Eddy was on a par with the Model-T Ford as a butt for jokes, and any man who had suggested such a thing as psychosomatic medicine they classed lower than the doctors who advertised themselves as restorers of lost manhood.

The corners of my abhorrence of the first three taboos had been somewhat worn off by my association with Mamie and the construction workers, but I still considered myself a Vestal Virgin protecting the holy fire of medicine from quacks, soothsayers and osteopaths. From childhood I had dreamed about Indians, of course, but I had never seen any except in the Buffalo Bill show. However, our old family doctor had once lived among them in the Oklahoma Territory. When making calls he drove a team of spotted Indian ponies and often took me along for the ride. He had been a boyhood friend of my father's, came from the same sod, voted the same ticket and was a Methodist by marriage, so what he said was gospel as far as I was concerned. He instilled a great sympathy in my breast for the poor downtrodden red man. Now that I was a doctor I determined to do all in my power to help these unfortunate people to enjoy the blessings of 1917-vintage medicine.

But the Gosiute felt no need for such blessings. He thought he was doing all right as he was. He was the original inhabitant of the welfare state. F.D.R. may have thought he himself invented it, but the Indian Bureau of the Department of the Interior in Washington had him beat a mile.

The Gosiutes had once been an independent people and rustled for their own food. Pickings on the desert were scarce, and their diet consisted of jack rabbits, ground squirrels, pine nuts and an occasional antelope or wild horse. When the 1849 migration to California began, the wagon trains passed through the middle of the Gosiutes' hunting grounds. All those horses and oxen wandering around were too great a temptation for their weak moral fibre to resist. The hardy pioneers retaliated by raping every squaw they could catch, shooting the bucks, and blaming their own thievery from other trains upon the Indians.

After some kindhearted soul had introduced the simple savage to the blessings of whisky, the plot was really set. The Overland stages hurried across Clifton Flats as fast as horse flesh could draw them, and passed through a hailstorm of arrows and stones from behind every rock or stunted juniper. Finally the Indians ganged up and attacked the stage station on the west side of Fish Springs Mountain. They set fire to the sheds, and when the men ran out to save the stock, clubbed them to death. Then they had a big horse and mule barbecue, drank all the whisky and behaved in a most ungrateful manner, considering everything that had been done for and to them.

About this time Col. Pat Conner's army arrived in Utah to show Brother Brigham that he was still in the United States and discourage his reported intention of founding an independent nation known as Deseret. That canny old ex-Methodist needed money more than he did independence, so he sold the invaders vegetables and meat at desert prices instead of wasting expensive ammunition in resisting them. There wasn't much of anything to do, so the army moved out into Tooele County and founded Camp Floyd. Half of the troops went over the hill and opened up many great mines in Stockton and Park City. The non-miners got pretty bored because the Mormon maids would have nothing to do with them, and everyone was happy when Washington ordered them on west to knock some manners into the pesky Gosiutes.

The surest way to achieve this end was to exterminate them, but Conner had an idea that if he just drove them out on the poorest country, starvation would produce the same result with less bother. He assigned the Skull Valley bunch a rocky hillside on the west slope of the Stansbury range, and moved the main tribe to the bench land at the western foot of Mt. Ibapah. It was so cold there that they could not raise gardens. Since they were not herdsmen, their end was assured if they stayed there.

Then some prehistoric New Dealer down Washington way insisted that they must be fed. Conner gave them some army bacon and promised that if they behaved themselves there would be more where that came from.

The Gosiutes were smarter than they looked. They knew a gravy train when they saw one. They all piled aboard this one, and let the Washington ravens worry about their welfare. Eventually an agent was assigned to them with instructions to uplift them and make them self-supporting.

The Gosiutes didn't take kindly to weaning. They toiled not, neither did they spin very fast over the years that followed. For a generation they loafed around the country and enjoyed themselves in a modest way, having an occasional fight with their cousins, the Paiutes of central Utah, and visiting with the Blackfeet in Idaho. They so successfully resisted all efforts to educate or put them to work that when the Indian Rights Society was organized back East, they became its shining light. Their medicine man was also the priest and delegate to any Indian congress which promised to put the bee on Washington for more grub, and as such was a bitter foe of the Indian agents.

This was the situation when I arrived. It was still operating when I left. I was so horrified at the laziness and shiftlessness of these people that when the alphabet boys began grinding out pie in the sky for everybody, I broke with family tradition, as well as my own brothers, and voted the Republican ticket—probably the first Peck in history so to disgrace the name.

The agent in charge at this time was an old time bureaucrat who worried more about his reports than about the Indians. In addition to his other duties he was busily trying to make the Gosiutes over into Ohio Presbyterians like the ones he had known back home. He hated them, and they returned the compliment. He was also desperately afraid of them and kept loaded guns scattered all over the agency residence.

His sister-in-law was supposed to be the schoolteacher, but nary an Indian ever darkened the door of her temple of learning in quest of an education. This schoolmarm once threw an old pair of high-heeled shoes on the garbage dump. A little Indian girl spied them, and like little girls everywhere, tried them on. There was ice on the ground, and such stilts on feet that had never known anything but buckskin moccasins

made for insecure footing. She promptly fell down and broke
her arm just above the wrist.

The medicine man was called. He howled all night, but his
racket did not straighten the arm. The child's mother sometimes helped the housewives down the valley, where she had
heard them discuss the white medicine man in Gold Hill. She
demanded that he be called.

The men all hooted at the idea, but even Gosiute women
had a habit of dominating their lords, and the agent was
asked to send for me. Here I glimpsed the key by which I
could unlock the door of ignorance and bring the blessings of
civilized medicine to the poor folks in this desert Macedonia.
I had great hopes for my fellow man, and like the youth of
all generations believed that I was anointed with the holy fire
to bring peace and understanding to the whole world.

I arrived at the Reservation after dark and stopped at the
agent's. He pulled down the blinds, locked the doors and
then sat down close beside me where we could converse in a
low tone. He painted a picture of these bloodthirsty savages
that made my hair curl. Before the agent got through briefing
me, I began to picture myself as that old saint whose body
was stuck so full of arrows that he resembled a porcupine.

The agent qualified himself by stating that he had been
engaged in this Indian agency work for years, and had known
many tribes in all parts of the country. The only reason he
was located in this hellish spot was that some supervisor had
it in for him, influenced no doubt by the Indian Rights
Society. He was staying on only until his retirement pay became effective.

I never did learn just who the members of the Indian
Rights Society were, or their function, except that they were
a band of dedicated Easterners who did not know Indians.
They apparently believed them all prototypes of the noble
Uncas of James Fenimore Cooper fame, and amused them-
selves with making life a hell for the Indian Department and

its field employees. If the Indians did not have a grievance, these people would think one up for them and cry and bleed all over the Eastern papers about the said plight of "Lo, the poor red man."

"Why, Doctor," the agent continued, "if you do not get a perfect result with that fracture, and the Indians do not scalp you first, in two weeks that child's picture will be on the front pages of all the Eastern papers captioned 'Little Indian girl disfigured for life by careless employee of the Indian Bureau.' What's more, the picture will be so doctored that the unfortunate child will look as if she could scratch her elbow with the hand attached to the same arm.

"Don't trust them for a minute. I warn you, an Indian is sneaky, treacherous, cruel, bloodthirsty, a liar and a beggar. Never let your guard down for a minute, but be ready to run or fight at all times.

"The ringleader of the opposition is their old medicine man. He is a devil and as sly as a fox. He is called Annie Tommy. That is not his tribal name as that is too obscene for white men to use. But his mother's name was Annie and his is Tommy, and as there are other Tommys in the tribe, he is called Annie Tommy. You will never get to see him in action because the treatment of the sick is a religious rite and as secret as the ritual of a fraternal lodge. But almost any night you can hear him singing at the top of his lungs at the door of a sick Indian or of one he wants to scare into line.

"They are all afraid of his magic and believe that he has a private telephone line to the Great Spirit, who does his bidding. They think their entering into heavenly bliss rests upon his recommendation. Why should they waste time depending on you to save them the inconveniences of the trip? You might fail, and then where would they be? Tonight he is, of course, making powerful medicine to insure your failure tomorrow. He considers my calling you an insult to his art, his religion and his professional reputation."

When I went to bed, about all the hope I had to cling to
was that another Pocahontas would appear to play opposite
my Captain John Smith. Considering the specimens of feminine pulchritude I had seen among the Indians when they
came to Gold Hill, however, I was a bit uncertain whether I
would prefer to be saved or suffer the tommyhawk and be
done with it.

As soon as daylight came, I slipped out of bed and went to
look over the field of operations. The patient was not to be
brought to the school house until nine A.M. Now was a good
time to map out a route for retreat should it be necessary.

The landscape was dismal enough to depress anyone. The
Reservation was on an alluvial fan cuddled up against the
foot of the high, precipitous slopes of Mt. Ibapah. It was bare
of everything except scrubby sagebrush and a little stream
flowing down the middle of it, the course of which was
marked by some stunted willow brush. Along this stream
were some fifty wickiups, and behind most of them, a dirt-
roofed log cabin. A few discouraged looking dogs wandered
about. Here and there stood a beat-up Ford touring car, or at
least the bare essentials of such a vehicle. None of them had
tops, windshields, lights, hoods, paint or spare tires. Close
inspection showed one accessory always present, a horn with
a big rubber bulb to squeeze when one wished to blow it. The
Indians evidently liked music. Smoke was coming out of the
tops of the wickiups, but none from the cabins.

I asked the agent, who now had joined me, about this peculiar circumstance. He reported that Washington (under
pressure from the Indian Rights Society) had decreed that
each family have a log cabin to live in when the weather was
cold—a snug little nest where they could gather around
the fire and read about Minnehaha and eat pine nuts on cold
winter evenings. The men had been paid wages to go up on
the mountain and cut logs and float or drag them down to the
building sites, where imported labor shaped and erected the

cabins. Each cabin cost the government about a thousand dollars. The Indians spent their earnings in a Nevada auto-wrecking yard for the cars parked beside their homes. They believed living in a house was unhealthy, and used them to store deer hides, sheep pelts, busted auto springs, saddles and other junk too bulky to keep in their living quarters, the wickiups.

We went into the school house, where the agent built a fire. I moved the teacher's table close to the door, where I could stand and be handy to the exit. The spectators would be hindered by the table if hostilities broke out. Then I moved my car out in front of the school and pointed it down the hill, which was steep enough for me to let gravity crank the thing should I feel compelled to leave hurriedly.

The patient arrived promptly, accompanied by the entire male population of the camp, some forty men and boys. They were a solemn looking bunch but not particularly awe-inspiring. Every man over twenty-five was as big around as he was tall. I felt better, for I didn't believe that, with all that tallow to carry, any of them could run thirty yards in less than five minutes. Still I was a bit alarmed to notice that the agent had moved his own car out on the road and stopped it down the hill ahead of mine. His wife and sister were sitting in it.

When I asked him about this maneuver, he said they were going to Deep Creek shopping as soon as I had finished. Oh well, every man for himself; if I beat him to it I would jump in his car and save the women, and let him navigate my own stubborn jalopy.

The Indians all crowded back of the table so thickly that some of them stood within a foot of the roaring stove, which was red hot by this time. They began to smell terrible.

I had planned to use ether for an anesthetic but gave it up for chloroform, which is more dangerous for the patient but does not explode so easily when the vapor comes in contact with fire. I knew I would not need much as the fracture was only a green stick type of the lower forearm, called in the old books a silver fork deformity.

Before I gave the child any anesthetic I tried the splints I had prepared on her good arm. Only then did a sound come from the spectators, a sort of a grunt which I suppose meant, "Look at the damned fool, he doesn't know which arm is broken." Not a smile or the batting of an eyelash. They just stood there like so many gobs of dough and wore the same animated expression.

I made one friend, however. All my life I had been able to warm up to little girls. As patients I loved them and could always talk them into being good sports and standing the hurt. I turned all my charm on this kid, and she responded nicely. We could not understand each other, but we could smile, and we did. After the Indian interpreter told her what I was going to do, she went to sleep like an angel.

A couple of flips and the deformity was corrected and the arm in splints. That blessed baby awoke with a smile for me and a torrent of words directed toward the spectators. I held up the bandaged arm for all to see. There wasn't a sign of emotion among any of them. They started to file out of the building, looking neither to the right nor the left, like a bunch of lodge brothers at a funeral. My ego went flop.

Just as the first man went through the door, the most awful howls began outside. I rushed to see the dog fight. It was only Annie Tommy himself, high priest, union leader, and local disciple of the god Aesculapius, calling down curses upon my unethical head. From the racket I imagined he was telling his gods that if they failed him now, they could expect no more business from him.

I walked out and offered my hand in professional fellowship, but he spurned it and stomped away from there, waving his staff and howling at the top of his lungs. The other Indians stood around admiring the fireworks and never favored me with a single glance.

The operation had been an anatomical success but a psychological failure. I had earned my fee and all I could do now was go home. Had they been after me with knives and hatchets, or even dented the car's body with an arrow or two, I would have been elated. But to be ignored is a big pill for a youngster to swallow. It is worse to be humbled by an old scarecrow, dressed in greasy Levis, a faded "Monkey-Ward" plaid shirt and a rag of a hat, with a moth-eaten blanket about his shoulders and triumph in his eye.

Must science bow to savage ignorance and bombast? To all appearances it had done just that. I realized that my failure to look him up the night before and show professional courtesy probably had not helped matters much. Now what could I do? Paint my face and howl right back at him, or preserve my professional dignity and retire from the field with my head bowed by a sense of failure?

There is nothing so stirring to the blood of the young as opposition. I knew that I must expect the same reaction, though perhaps not so violent and spectacular, from civilized white doctors once I came into competition with them. I honestly admired the man's reactions more than had he offered me the fishy hand of professional friendship which I would have to learn to accept and to dish out myself in similar circumstances. So it was to be war, fought to the finish in a struggle for men's minds. I was determined to steal his practice and win these Indians' confidence, and I used all the tricks for which my profession was famous to unseat him. I am sure he returned the compliment.

Medicine did not always come out the victor. The medicine man was a specialist in prognosis. From what I could learn, he didn't bother with diagnosis or administration of remedies, but when he told an Indian his time had come, that Indian went right home, crawled into his wickiup and stayed there until the Great Spirit was ready to receive him.

Willie was a boy of about seventeen who hung around the

agency quite a bit and could talk fair English. I got in the habit of letting him ride up the canyon with me when I was through at the clinic I had established, and I wanted to catch a few trout to take home for supper.

One afternoon he wasn't there. I drove by his teepee to see if he wanted to go, and was met at the entrance by his mother, who looked as if there had been a death in the family.

"Where is Willie?" I asked.

She shook her head mournfully. "Pretty soon Willie die."

I pushed by her. Willie was lying upon a blanket-covered pile of straw looking about as healthy as ever.

When I asked him what was the matter, he replied that Annie Tommy had said he was going to die. They had sent for their relatives in Skull Valley, so he guessed he was.

I examined that boy carefully, sent his sputum to the State Board of Health for T.B. examination asking them to use guinea pig inoculation as well as microscopic tests, did blood counts and everything else I could think of to find something wrong with him. I made several extra trips to the Reservation at my own expense to check his temperature, but I never did find a damned thing the matter with that kid. He didn't even lose much weight. But pretty soon Willie did die.

Did that old bastard put the hex on the boy because Willie was friendly toward me, or did he just want to show me that his medicine was of a much more powerful muzzle velocity than my own?

After he had had a few such triumphs over my therapy, I concluded the old devil was slipping our patients a medicinal Mickey Finn. These suspicions were, I am now sure, unwarranted. He fought fair and held to his own system of practice, handed down to him through generations of medicine men, no doubt. It just happened that he was an expert in a branch of the healing art of which I had never been informed by my teachers. Jenner learned about smallpox vaccination from the milk-maids; digitalis and quinine were borrowed from savage tribes; and I had Annie Tommy to thank for a course in psychosomatic medicine ten years before anything about it appeared in the medical journals.

12

Washington and I

My visits to the Gosiutes created a very different atmosphere in our nation's capital than was apparent on the Ibapah Reservation.

As soon as the vouchers reached the bureaucrats and they realized that there was a doctor within driving distance of the Indians, they put Plan B to work and demanded that I hold at least two clinics per month at the agency, spending half of the period on a well-baby clinic. That was all the Gosiutes needed for a womb to tomb set-up. They had been forced to pay Howler in pine nuts and squirrels, but now everything was free but gasoline and whisky.

When I read the directive, I remarked to the agent that I would be taking money under false pretenses. I was tempted. It meant fifty dollars twice a month, a cabin assigned to me at the agency, and expenses. Where else could a man get two fishing and hunting trips a month and be paid for it? Besides it would give me a chance to tilt with the old medicine man on a regular schedule. I guess association with the Indians, and the high altitude, weakened my moral fibre. I was on hand for the first scheduled clinic.

I had requisitioned a supply of canned milk and cod liver oil because the Indians were in the habit of feeding the babies black ant soup and Arbuckle's coffee once the natural food supply was exhausted. The old girls back in Washington were very anxious to hear about the babies gaining weight. About a carload of this baby ration arrived. As soon as the ladies of the tribe heard about something new being offered for free, they came running.

At the first clinic I saw fifteen babies, though according to the agent's count there were only six kids in the place under five years of age. Any mother who would not have loaned out her cub for purposes so laudable as fleecing Uncle Sam out of a few more groceries would have been considered unneighborly to say the least.

I fixed that little game by branding each kid behind the ear with a spot of methylene-blue dye which would be hard to wash off if, on an unlikely chance, the mother decided to bathe the baby. When that little ringer appeared again in another woman's arms—or, rather, on her back—I looked for my brand and refused any more milk for that day.

Then each baby seemed to develop an awful appetite, and I was asked to dish out several quarts a day for his nourishment. I had to give all my directions through the Indian interpreter, of course, and I suspected him of helping the girls think up schemes to fleece the government through me.

When the babies showed no great improvement on this bountiful diet, I was a bit puzzled as to what was becoming of it. Then one day I happened to stop in at the sagebrush saloon just across the Nevada line. There, piled up in the rear, were about five cases of government canned milk. Upon inquiry I learned that the Indians traded the milk for whisky. The saloon keeper sold the milk to the Deep Creek store, where the sheepherders and ranchers were happy to buy it at the reduced price which still made the store and saloon keepers a profit.

Here was a switch. Instead of trade, not aid, we had aid initiating trade. Everybody was prospering from the canned milk but the babies.

We had to show a gain on the baby charts, so I took the easy way and like the butchers weighed my hand when the red line seemed too flat. It took about a half hour to unlace a baby from his tote board, so I weighed a few boards and averaged them up and thereafter weighed baby and all and deducted the tare.

This practice got me into another mess. One little girl baby looked so undernourished that I had the mother strip her. After examining her carefully I could find no cause of her disability but undernourishment. Fixing up a bottle of formula, I fed her myself. The kid grabbed it as though she were starving. I scolded the mother as best I could through a third party and ordered her back on the next clinic day, informing her that Uncle Sam would be unhappy if she did not feed that baby and make her strong.

They did not show up until the second clinic a month later. The baby had made a wonderful improvement. I called the agent to see the change, and he sat right down to write Washington about it. Wanting to check the gain carefully, I ordered the baby stripped for accurate weighing. The kid was a boy.

Jimmy Clover, the interpreter, waved his arms and talked Gosiute a while. Then he turned to me.

"She say her baby die," he said. "She didn't want your Uncle Sam to feel bad, so she borrowed her sister's baby. They here visiting from Skull Valley."

Dealing with those simple savages was more fun than poker. They would think up a new game, and I would try to call their hand. We all enjoyed it immensely. But the benefit to the babies was nil.

The men were not quite so cute. I quickly found out that they would drink anything out of a bottle so long as it was red. One day I gave a man some drug—I have forgotten what it was—dissolved in simple syrup with a bit of red coloring. Simple syrup is about 110-proof. The first swallow tasted so good to him that he drank the whole four ounces as soon as he was out of the building. Then he spread the glad tidings.

Within an hour there were four more bucks in the clinic suffering from the same set of symptoms the first man had complained of, and demanding some of that red medicine. I had a saturated solution of epsom salts made up, so I colored that red and gave each a bottle. Then I watched through the window to see the result. They all uncorked their bottles and took a long swig as soon as they reached the yard. For once I saw an Indian show surprise.

It made me more work, however. They did not blame the joke on me, but ganged up on the discoverer of this nectar and beat him up so badly that I had to repair the damage to his face.

When Washington wanted a picture of the little Gosiutes, I waited until the Skull Valley tribe were over visiting. I borrowed all their infants, which added to our own, made a nice group photograph. Indians are not given to posing for a photographer, believing it some kind of bad luck, but the expectation of more rations of milk negotiable at the Nevada saloon overcame their scruples.

I have no idea who was in charge of the baby department of the Indian Bureau in Washington, but because of their deep interest in other people's babies and their willingness to direct the raising of them, I concluded that they must be a gang of frustrated old maids bent upon satisfying their own thwarted maternal instincts by telling other people how to raise their kids. This opinion was strengthened during the war. I was listed as a volunteer from this department and so received a box of presents and had my name engraved on a tablet in the Department of the Interior building.

In that box were several pairs of home knit socks and sweaters. They were weird. One pair of socks had feet twenty-four inches long and two and one half inches wide, and legs only three inches high. Some of my evil-minded companions suggested that they were supposed to keep another part of my body warm instead of my feet. If so, I appreciated the compliment, but I still believe that they were meant for umbrella covers. It was all I could do, when sending in my reports from Ibapah, to keep from heading them "Dear Aunt Hetty."

Perhaps it was well that there was somebody taking this baby welfare campaign in earnest. I could not convince the Indians of its importance, and some place down inside me I felt that the Indians were right.

Here were a people of most limited resources, subject to unbelievable hardships over generations of time, trained to a life that allowed no coddling of the weak and where only the fittest survive. Had not Mother Nature, in her wisdom, taught these mothers that the sickly and deformed child was bound to suffer untold hardships and fall by the trail at last, so that it was better that he be taken in infancy and all the suffering and disappointments avoided? Are we white people more humane in saving every unfortunate and condemning him to a life of suffering and frustration, homes for the feeble-minded, asylums and the like? Is a life of pain and disappointment better than a merciful oblivion before the child develops a thinking brain?

This question has put more gray hairs on the heads of obstetricians than any other emergency in the art. You look down at the poor tiny misshapen chunk of animate clay and shiver at the thought that it is within your power to neglect some little thing and allow this mistake to be obliterated. Or should you endeavor to save this life and condemn it to a period of hell on earth? No man has ever lived long enough to know the answer. Were these Gosiute women wiser than I when they traded the milk for whisky and let the unfit die? They were good mothers, kind and gentle with their children. Were they also kind in eliminating the weak that the tribe might be perpetuated only by the strong?

My Hippocratic oath and medical ethics left me no choice but to struggle against their natural wisdom. I divided my time in cursing their stubbornness and laughing at their schemes to tap my supply of goods that could be exchanged for liquids of more immediate effect.

I never did learn much about Annie Tommy's Great Spirit or the religion of these Indians. Their yearly binges upon marijuana and peote had somewhat the nature of a religious festival. When questioned about it they always said it was too long and complicated to explain to a white man and we would not understand, a conclusion that was probably true.

I did learn about one of their fables, however, a mixture of Washington Irving and the Kilkenny cats. It seemed that many generations ago the Gosiutes got into a war with some tiny men who lived up on Ibapah mountain. The battle lasted a generation or two until finally they decided that nobody could win. A truce was called and an agreement was made. It had been kept ever since. The Gosiutes were to have the territory in the day time but must leave the mountain before darkness when the little men took over.

The mountain was very steep, and rock slides down the slopes were common, particularly in winter. The roar from them could be plainly heard at the Reservation. I was told that mothers gathered their children around them at these times and told them that the noise and rumbles came from the little men playing up on the mountain. Their favorite sport seemed to be rolling rocks down the canyon walls. The kids were properly impressed with the danger to any Gosiute who ventured up there after dark.

While fishing I camped many nights on the slopes of this mountain, and never saw an Indian up there after dark. Whether the legend was believed by all the tribe I do not know. Perhaps it was an excuse for the bucks to remain at home instead of getting out and hunting as their wives insisted they do.

My practice among the Gosiutes was confined to men and children with only one major exception, the wife of the interpreter. She could be expected to call the doctor who was responsible for her husband's job. This lack of women patients was not very good preparation for my future professional life in which, as is the case with a general practitioner in all civilized communities, eighty percent of my patients would be female.

Later in my career I met a physician who had done Indian practice during the period of which I write. He was the only other doctor I knew who had been called to treat an Indian woman. Strangely enough, this was also the first and only time I ever heard of a physician and a medicine man reaching an agreement upon diagnosis and disposition.

Over in Skull Valley, one of the Moon boys had gone up into Idaho to some kind of Indian fraternal convention. He had a high old time, and when he came back to earth three days later, he discovered, much to his surprise, that he had acquired a wife somewhere along his recent primrose path. He felt no need for a wife, but he didn't know just how to shake her. What's more, she was a daughter of the tribe who were hosts of the clambake. It wouldn't look right for one who had accepted their hospitality to refuse to relieve them of this burden. So he brought her home and moved in with his folks.

This was a mistake. Some mothers and daughters-in-law have succeeded in living in the same state or even the same town, but such a combination in a teepee, ten feet across at its widest diameter, is impossible. Within a couple of days the girl began to act as a no-good Gosiute should. She spent her time sitting in the middle of the wickiup, howling at the top of her lungs and pulling handfuls of hair out of her scalp.

Annie Tommy was called from Ibapah. He diagnosed evil spirits and ordered her sent home to her folks as inferior goods. The girl, however, had been raised in a tribe who were used to white physicians, and she demanded a white doctor. My friend answered the call.

He said the poor thing seemed half frightened to death, and he did not blame her. The mother-in-law was stomping around the tent, emitting grunts like the snorts of a bull moose and continually sharpening a knife upon a strip of buckskin that hung from her waist. My friend sized up the situation quickly and agreed with Annie Tommy that there were evil spirits thereabouts. Thinking it easier to get rid of the girl than the mother-in-law, he advised that the bride be returned to her people.

In later years a dear old Mormon midwife gave me a description of the birth process among the Gosiutes. She had lived near them in Skull Valley and had been allowed to attend one of these coming-out parties in her younger days.

When the stork made known his coming, the prospective mother and an older woman went off into the brush and stayed there until junior made his appearance. The mother delivered the babe in the squatting position. As the baby's head emerged, she fell forward upon her hands and knees. The older woman pushed her over on her back and cut the cord. She wrapped the loose end around her hand a time or two and gave a mighty jerk, at the same time stamping on or kicking the mother's belly with her moccasin-covered foot. That completed the operation, and everybody went home.

Of course, that is the position taken by all savage women at a time like this. It would be assumed by white women except for the fact that doctors cannot sit on a stool during such a procedure, and doctors are prone to sit rather than stand.

Like other savage tribes Indians have babies with small and easily moulded heads. It is only the white race that develops big-headed boys and makes the birth process more complicated.

Sometimes things went wrong for these daughters of nature. In a female skeleton that was unearthed during the excavations for Lake Mead a babe's head was caught with its chin wedged behind the pelvic bones of the mother. This would have been no complication for a physician, as he could have rotated the head to a normal breech position and delivered the infant easily. But there were no DeLees around at that time, and a medicine man's howling would only have added to the horror and hopelessness of the poor mother. The baby must have died quickly. Let us hope they batted the mother over the head with a rock, as death for her then was inevitable and of long time coming and the time was all anguish.

I did not get to practice obstetrics on the Gosiutes. What bothered me most was my inability to talk directly to a mother when advising her about her baby's feeding problems. An interpreter, and a man at that, is not likely to transmit a doctor's directions in very great detail.

Not long after my wife's arrival I discovered that she could converse with the Indian women with no trouble at all. I was almost sure that she had known no word of Gosiute when she arrived, and I could not understand how she became proficient in so short a time. Finally I insisted that Jimmy Clover give me the lowdown on this situation. Then I was sorry I had brought up the subject as Jimmy's account lent little glory to my own sex and race.

Jimmy said that a long time ago when the first white men came through this region they attacked the Indian women as though they were animals. The tribal wise men decreed that Gosiute women should hide whenever they saw white men in the neighborhood, and if they were caught should act as uncommunicative as possible. They also were advised to grab a handful of gravel and insert it where it would dull the ardor of the predatory white men. Jimmy did not give me that last bit of folklore for like all other Indians he was reticent about sex matters. It was told me by an old prospector who seemed to know what he was talking about. But Jimmy did say that all the Gosiute women actually understood English perfectly.

The hardy winners of the West were a cut or two below their red brothers. I never heard of a Gosiute man in this region attacking a white woman at any time.

Jimmy's wife was from some other tribe. Several times she almost forgot the taboo and started to speak to me when I stopped to pick up her husband before making calls around the camp. But she always caught herself in time. I never met a white man who had been directly addressed by a Gosiute woman.

Jimmy and his wife were different in other ways from the general run of Gosiutes. They lived in their cabin and used the wickiup for a store room. The cabin had curtains at the windows, and was spotlessly clean whenever Jimmy invited me in. That cabin was to be the scene of my greatest struggle in nearly forty years of medical practice. Jimmy came to Gold Hill in search of me one evening, reporting that his wife was suffering from severe abdominal pains. He was afraid her appendix had burst or something of the kind.

I took my microscope and blood counting chamber and drove to his cabin at once. She was in pain all right, and in the proper place, but the blood count was normal. Yet she was breathing fast, and her pulse was racing and weak. They had no children at the time, but Jimmy said there was reason to suppose that she was pregnant.

I agreed with the supposition, but realized that the pregnancy was in a tube and that the tube had ruptured. She was having an internal hemorrhage. This is a hard thing to explain to an Indian when there is no blood evident. The ideal treatment was, of course, to open the abdomen, tie off the bleeding vessel and remove the tube and ovum. But how near could I come to that idea with no help of any experience closer than a hundred and fifty miles, and few instruments to use in the operation?

I was faced with a decision. Should I attempt the operation, or sit on my hands and hope that nature and the Indian Great Spirit would combine to stop that bleeder before the woman died of hemorrhage? It was a battle. Inaction is hard for the young. And, believe me, a man can feel pretty forlorn when he comes up against the problem of a human life and has not even a nurse to talk it over with.

I was influenced in my final decision by recalling a motto in DeLee's *Maternity*. It was in Latin, and I hate Latin phrases in a book, but it meant in English: "If you are not sure of helping the patient, don't do anything to harm her."

So I tilted up the foot of the bed, put a hot water bottle full of snow on her belly, and quieted her with some morphine. Then I went outside in the hope that, as it did the Psalmist, looking up at the hills might give me strength.

It seemed that there must be a difference between lifting one's eyes to the hills and gazing up at a mountain, because old Mt. Ibapah never looked so unfriendly. It was a bright moonlight night, and that vast expanse of snow and rocks towering above me was as unresponsive as any landscape could be. While I stood there I heard the muffled roar of a rock slide, and like the children in the teepees I shivered and felt more useless and insignificant than at any other time in my life.

Howler was away at a union convention of the Indian Rights Society, and I sure missed him and his music. In fact,

I would have gladly gone out and joined in the howling on the off chance that his Great Spirit might be attracted to an unfamiliar voice and listen to my supplications. It was a night of a thousand hours. I spent most of it standing in the doorway looking up at that repellent old mountain. I have never liked mountains since.

Once an hour I would check her blood pressure and pulse. The one was descending slowly and the other rising, as the heart had to work faster to circulate the remaining blood within her veins. About three o'clock they stopped their fluctuations. For the next hour I held my breath, hoping against hope that the bleeding vessel had clotted.

By six A.M. there was still no sign of progression of the hemorrhage. I inserted needles beneath her breasts and injected some salt solution of the same salinity as the blood. I had invaded the agency and collected all the hot water bottles I could find and boiled the solution for this possibility.

When the sun finally climbed up the other side of Mt. Ibapah and shone upon this little cabin in the sagebrush it was greeted by a happy man. My patient's condition was improved. She was awake and spoke a few words to her husband.

When I explained the situation to Jimmy Clover as best I could, he casually remarked: "Oh, she know all about it. She hear you talking to yourself in the night. She used to work for a doctor in the Indian hospital in Carson City and knows about blood counts and what was wrong with her. She say thank you for being so nice."

There is nothing that makes a man so happy as having events justify his judgment, especially when a life is saved thereby. Neither before nor since has the world looked so good to me as it did that morning.

I stayed at her bedside for the next two days. Then Jimmy and I filled a truck half full of sacks of rocks to make the springs soft, loaded her on a pallet which rested upon the sacks, and took her to Wendover, where we caught a train to Salt Lake City. There, with a good man at my elbow, her abdomen was opened and enormous clots and the offending tube were removed.

She made an uneventful recovery and in after years presented Jimmy with three fine children. They often stopped at our home when they were out selling pine nuts to the white people in the eastern part of the country.

One incident connected with the case still makes me sore. When we arrived at Wendover I had the trainmen load her stretcher through the window into a Pullman berth. I wanted her kept as quiet as possible in fear that the clot might become dislodged, causing her to bleed again. The government refused to pay for that Pullman fare. It said such frills were not allowable in transporting sick Indians. I had to foot the bill myself, in addition to my own expenses.

That little stunt eased my conscience many times in later years when I caught myself giving Uncle Sam the small end of the bargain in WPA days.

13

Indian Charley

When a man works hard at a thing, he likes to see some progress. If I made any impression upon this tribe of savages, it was not revealed unto me. They apparently grew to like me in their undemonstrative way, but accepting me as a physician was another matter. They recognized my superior ability in repairing wounds and setting broken bones, but in all serious afflictions such as T.B. and other major diseases I was only a somewhat noisy nuisance to their medicine man. All I got out of the experience was a better understanding of my own race and a more tolerant attitude toward their Gosiute-like actions.

Under the skin we are all Gosiutes, with our traditions, our general superstition, our fears of the unknown. Perhaps that is why Indian Charley was my pride and joy. He was a representative of that great class who send away for youth restorer and blood builder, and are quick to desert their old family physician for any bone cracker who comes along and promises pie in the sky, either medicinal or political.

Charley was willing to try anything new that was offered him, an attitude that makes America tick and the TV companies rich. The personification of non-conformity and an expert on "brinkmanship," Charley was a member of the tribal council but was hardly ever in agreement with his fellows. He was respected by his white brothers, damned by the tribal priest-medicine man and certain high officers of the

U.S. Army, and loved by the privates of that Army. He supplied me with more real belly laughs than ten Bob Hopes.

The Indian Rights Society and the Gosiutes had been in the hair of bureaucratic Washington so long that violent measures were contemplated to cut their umbilical cord and set them adrift as ordinary landholders rather than wards of the government. An old boyhood acquaintance of mine by the name of Trotter, who was high up in the Bureau of Indian Affairs, came out to Deep Creek to see what could be done. He advised the purchase of all the farming land in the valley, settling the Indians upon it and letting them work for their living.

He received an O.K. from Washington, but before closing the deal with the farmers he decided he had better get the Gosiute reaction to the plan. A meeting was called of the tribal council for him to present the plan and ask for approval. He did not get it. These Indians were way ahead of their time.

Antelope Jake was their spokesman. His talk was relayed to me by Mr. Trotter: "The Gosiutes do not like to think of all their white friends and neighbors moving out of the valley. We love them and would be unhappy should they leave. You say this plan would cost many thousands of dollars. We say, just give us the money and we stay right here. Be a lot less trouble for everybody."

Charley jumped up and offered a minority report, stating that he would like a farm of his own and was not afraid to work it. How Secretary of Agriculture Benson would have loved him! Charley was, of course, overruled by the majority. The agent reported that the Gosiute were not ready for rugged individualism. (In these later days it seems that their philosophy has become popular.)

Charley showed his disdain for tribal customs by going down into the valley and hiring out to a rancher who was putting up hay. While he was raking alfalfa, his horses became frightened at a hornets' nest, and ran away. Charley wound up with a rake tooth through his arm.

I was over Callao way on a baby case when the accident happened and did not get to Charley until the next afternoon. When I arrived, Howler was in charge. All the relatives had gathered around to see Charley climb the golden stair.

I'd had enough. Either I took care of Charley as I saw fit, or these Indians would be treated to a lively fight between their medicine men. The relatives were all confident that "pretty soon Charley die," and resisted my interference. But when I put it up to Charley, he said: "You do what you want, Doc, but get me out of here so I won't have to listen to that old devil yelling me into hell."

I was dumb enough in those days to think the disease was the extent of my responsibility. That remark opened up the whole problem of Howler's success—the power of mind over matter. His control over them amounted to playing upon their superstitious awe of anything they did not understand. To save Charley I had to get him out of there and away from this evil influence.

I went right to the agent and demanded authority to take Charley to the Fort Douglas Hospital in Salt Lake City because of the severity of his wound. The agent agreed. Charley's wife cut up a lot of didoes, and Doc Howler turned on all his surplus lung power, but Charley was a man of his word. I dressed the wound, placed the arm in splints, and put Charley in my car for the drive to Wendover. All of this took time. It was nine P.M. when we reached Gold Hill. There I stopped and gave Charley some tetanus antitoxin and a swallow of snake bite preventative to make the ride more comfortable for him.

There is nothing so monotonous as driving on a salt flat at night. Nothing to see, no hills or valleys, no bridges to miss, no other cars to dodge. You just sit and watch the ground slide by under the feeble glare of the car's headlights. I had worked all the night before, and Charley had suffered a lot of pain plus the misery of listening to the medicine man. We promptly went to sleep.

How long we slept I do not know, but when I awoke, the Silver Zone mountains, which should have been on our left, were on our right. I could see their summits against the starlit sky. Either we had turned around or we were clear across the valley and these peaks were the Skull Valley range. Lost, smack in the middle of the desert with a sick Indian!

I awakened Charley and asked him if he knew where he was. He replied, "Who cares?" showing that the snake bite remedy was something of a tranquilizer.

I cared. I wanted to get him on the eastbound train, which was due in Wendover shortly after midnight. The only stars I knew were those that make up the Big Dipper, and Polaris, but they were enough for me to do a bit of celestial navigation. I found that we had turned completely around and were headed back toward Gold Hill. On the road home a day later I traced our tracks; we had made a circle of about ten miles and were within a half mile of our starting point when I awoke.

When we reached the Denver and Rio Grande Station in Salt Lake City, the ambulance had not yet come. Charley informed me that he was going out behind the house to attend the calls of nature. I told him that there wasn't any behind to this house, that we would have to go to the men's room. We went, but Charley had his misgivings. He asked me to keep watch while he was occupied, for if anybody caught us we sure would land in jail for doing things like that in the house. The mystery of modern plumbing was beyond his understanding at that time.

When the army ambulance finally arrived, I turned Charley over to the soldiers and caught a freight train back to Wendover.

The next part of this chronicle was told me by a hospital

orderly whom I met at Fort Riley, Kansas, a few months later. He had been on the ward when Charley entered the hospital in Salt Lake City. The doctors ordered Charley to bed rest and no bathroom privileges, so the first task was to get him to bed and teach him the technique of using a bed pan. This he refused to do, even after one of the orderlies had undressed and got into the next bed to demonstrate the procedure. After two days Charley was allowed to wander about the ward as he saw fit.

Charley had never heard a brass band. When the regimental musicians practiced in a grove not far from the hospital, Charley sneaked off to see what made those pleasant sounds. The band boys liked him at once. When they stopped to moisten the reeds on the saxophones, and their own vocal cords, they passed the bottle to Charley. He became a real music fan.

Charley got along fine. He could have been released, but this was a government institution and the patient was having such a good time that the men did not call attention to his recovery. So Charley wandered about at will and worried only because they made him wear a hospital robe and kept his pants locked up.

One evening there was to be a review and parade at retreat. Since the big brass were there for an inspection of the Post, the band boys did not take on so much lubricant as usual. They gave Charley half a bottle of Panther Milk to polish off all by himself. He slept awhile. When he awoke to refresh himself and heard the stirring strains of "The Star-Spangled Banner" coming from the parade ground, his impulse was to get over to his friends on the off chance that they might have some more spare hooch. He acted upon it at once. Without taking time to fasten his bathrobe he started on the run for the grandstand.

The bathrobe had been made by some dame who thought all men are tall and slender. Charley was short and fat. Although there was plenty of bathrobe trailing on the ground behind him as he ran, there was also a lot of bare Indian sticking out in front. Such a spectacle upset the big brass a lot, as their ladies were among the guests.

The M.P.'s corralled Charley and took him to the hospital security ward. He was too drunk to care at the time, but when he sobered up and found himself restrained to quarters he became very sad indeed. The kindhearted orderlies realized that a cage was no place for this wild thing. They asked the officer of the day if they could not give Charley his pants: perhaps he would go over the hill. As soon as darkness came, Charley shook the dust of that hospital off his feet and, by some homing instinct common in wild things, got back to the Denver and Rio Grande Depot.

When he showed up in Gold Hill two days later he told me of his return trip. He had met some bums in the railway yards who directed him to a freight train going west on the Western Pacific and helped him into an empty box car. Next morning he asked permission to work his passage to Gold Hill on the Deep Creek Cannonball. Recognizing him as one of my patients, the conductor allowed him to ride free, and the brakeman gave him the remains of his lunch.

Charley was pretty dirty, but happy to get back. I drove him over to the Reservation in my car, and made a point of going by Howler's place to be sure he saw that his intended corpse was alive and kicking. Charley's wound was all healed, but I warned him to go to bed and get some rest. Then I went on up the canyon to see how the fish were biting.

I caught just enough for my supper. Then, deciding to stay all night and get the dawn fishing, I got out my bed roll and went to sleep. Within an hour or so I heard someone calling. I raised up on my elbows and answered. Pretty soon a couple of scared Indian boys showed up. Charley, they reported, had shot Annie Tommy, and the agent had said I must come right away.

I took them into my car so that no little men would harm them in the dark of Ibapah canyon, and returned to the agency.

My cup was running over. My business competitor was yelling for me louder than any of his patients ever had.

I examined the old man and found a nice twelve-gauge pattern of No. 4 shot decorating his rear exposure. They had ruined his pants, but none of the pellets had gone farther than the deeper layers of his skin and subcutaneous fat. Before I began playing "she loves me, she loves me not" on his rumble seat, I offered him some anesthetic. He refused it. I draped him over a barrel and started to work by the light of a smoky old lantern. Gently as I worked, I realized that he was not enjoying the procedure.

It took me a couple of hours to pick out all the shot. Then I painted the field with tincture of iodine and advised him not to sit down for a little while. That advice was not strictly necessary, but I had to say something to keep from laughing. Even a snicker at this time would make him my sworn enemy for life.

The agent was all excited and wanted to call the sheriff but I coaxed him to hold a trial himself and then let the thing drop. Nobody was seriously injured, and the less said about it the less harm done. So bright and early court was convened in the school house. The agent sat behind my operating table, looking stern and judicial. The plaintiff was defiantly standing at the bar. Most of the population of the Reservation were crowded into the rest of the courtroom.

Annie Tommy testified through Jimmy Clover, the interpreter, that he had just gone to welcome the invalid home, when without cause said defendant had up and shot him. Then it was time for Charley to tell his story. He disdained using Jimmy's services and substituted Army English for the kind used in the valley.

"Sure, I shot the sonofabitch," he said. "I had been pretty

sick, and if I listen to him I been dead two moons. Doc Peck bring me home last night and say Charley you tired, go to bed and sleep till sun comes up, you feel better. Just when I get to sleep that old bastard begin to howl right at side wickiup. I holler shut up and he holler louder. I say, 'Goddam you, I shoot you if you no shut up.' Wife say, 'No, Charley, he tell Great Spirit.' I say, 'To hell with Great Spirit and Annie Tommy too, I want to sleep.' Pretty soon he howl again. I get up, grab gun, and go out. It moonlight and I see him running toward barbed wire fence. I wait till he get in fence, maybe hundred steps away, and when he crawl through I fill his ass with bird shot. Next time he come howling around I use buck shot."

The agent broke in. "But, Charley, don't you know that he was just trying to help you?"

Charley snorted. "He never help anybody, only to die. He die doctor. Doc Peck he *live* doctor. Me, I want to live. Tommy's medicine no good. I tell about it to soldiers. They say all bushwah. Charley think so too."

The judge was coughing and blowing his nose, and the tears were dripping from his eyes in the great effort he had to put forth to maintain his dignity. His charge was delivered to both parties: "Tommy, don't you go there any more."

To this Tommy replied in good English, "Do you think I'm a damned fool?"

To Charley the judge said: "Don't you ever use that gun on anybody again. If you do, I'll call sheriff and take you to big jail. If Tommy bothers you any more you come and tell me."

Charley answered rather tartly, "I'll shoot him first and tell you after."

Court was dismissed. I had missed my morning's fishing, but I didn't much care.

I had accomplished my desire to drag my medical adver-

sary in the dirt, but victory was not very sweet. I felt sorry
for him and tried hard to become friends. I visited him several times to dress his wound, and sat around and talked as
cordially as I knew how. I even offered my sympathy for his
misfortune. But it made him madder than ever. I had gained
a point and scientific medicine was vindicated, but to what
purpose? I didn't want his damned practice even if I did get
it.

It was a catastrophe in his life, but it was a lucky turn for
me. It forewarned me that most of my white patients' illnesses would be the result of suggestion. It might be something they read, something someone said to them or something that happened in the neighborhood. As Dr. Cabot used
to say about heart disease, eight out of ten people who come
in suffering from heart disease don't have anything wrong
with their hearts.

I remember a case where a man who worked in a gang at
the smelter died of coronary disease. I made a bet with my
associate that we would see at least five members of that gang
within a week, all of them suffering from chest pains. I was
wrong, there were seven. Man was born to be fearful of the
unknown. A lot of doctors kill people by acting mysterious
about telling them what is the matter.

When a man pays a consultation fee he is entitled to know
what is in his doctor's mind. Perhaps the doctor is not sure
and does not want to be caught with a wrong diagnosis. Better he make a few mistakes than have just one man settle
up his affairs and get ready to die like Tommy's patients
among the Gosiutes.

I thought the case was closed, but a year later while I was
in the army a big bundle of correspondence came to me from
the Department of the Interior. Annie Tommy had reported
me for going fishing when I should have been available when
he got shot. He had requested the White Father to see to it

that I tended to business in the future. To clinch it, he had signed his tribal name and had got all the other council members to endorse it excepting, of course, Charley.

I enjoyed that letter ever so much and only regretted that the old ladies down in Washington did not understand Gosiute. When a baby was born into this tribe, if he came in an unusual position, he was named for the part of his body that first came into the world. Tommy had been born a breech, with his feet tucked up under his aftercoming chin. So he should have been named for the part that Charley shot at.

14

War and Peace

One would hardly believe a pistol shot that killed a second-rate duke in the Balkans would have reverberations in such a distant and isolated spot as the Ibapah Indian Reservation, but it did. And once again the Indian acted with the dignity which comes naturally to all wild things but which seems to decrease in direct ratio to the advancement of civilization.

For once I did not perform the functions of the goat in this charade. Washington relieved me of this task. However, my skirts were not entirely clean. I was forced to play a tank town version of Mata Hari, and to make it worse I did it for money, just as she did. If I was taking the king's shilling, I had to do as the king directed.

In the summer of 1917, when the draft was first put into effect, I had enlisted, but because the training camps for doctors were limited I had to wait a year before I was called. Being located in the middle of the desert, I was directed to examine all the draftees of the region, and I made several trips to various points to accommodate them. I was also under contract to care for the Gosiute Indians. When the three or four boys of draft age at the Reservation received greetings from the Draft Board, I was ordered to go over there and examine them.

These Indians had never achieved citizenship. They were carried as wards of the Indian Department. Probably they never would have been disturbed if the agent had not developed a patriotic brainstorm and insisted to the Department that these boys be called to serve the country to which they owed so little.

This turn of events was just what old Doc Annie Tommy wanted. He left hurriedly for the Blackfoot Reservation in Idaho, and reported everything to the Indian Grievance Committee. They wired the Indian Rights Society in New York, and Uncle Sam had another war on his hands. It was a war fought only with typewriters. Most of the bullets came from those staunch guardians of the Indians' rights, the Manhattan tribe.

I do not think they were particularly interested in the plight of the red man, but were crusaders by nature. The Gosiute was far enough away from them to gain their sympathy, and not close enough to display the other side of the coin.

The Department had been harassed to a point of desperation by their yapping. It decided to take a stand and get those Indians into uniform if it took the whole might of the country to accomplish it.

The first skirmish was my responsibility. Frankly I thought it all nonsense and believed the Indians were right in refusing to help the U.S.A. out of its difficulties with the Germans. But fifty dollars was fifty dollars, and I went over to examine the youth of Ibapah.

Just as I expected, none of them showed up. It was reported that they were all out sheepherding, an activity that was foreign to a Gosiute's nature and not a very likely story. The agent was raving about calling the sheriff and stomping around so much that I left him to boil and went to call upon my old friend and tribal wise man, Antelope Jake.

Jake was about eighty years old. He smoked a bag of Bull Durham per day in homemade cigarettes, always wore a vest made out of antelope skin with the hair outside, and was the spokesman and leader of the tribal council. He welcomed me graciously for an Indian, and came to the point at once by acknowledging that he was greatly worried.

I tried to bring him up to date on events and explain why the boys must go, but he just shook his head. "Jake no savvy why Americans have to go so far to fight. How come you know Germans well enough to get mad at them? Who are they and where do they live?"

I explained that we were mad because they sunk our ships in the ocean.

Jake replied, "Whose ocean is it anyhow?"

I said it belongs to everybody.

"Well," said Jake, "why not keep our boats at home until the war quiets down? What did the people on the other side have that we needed?"

That one floored me. I fell back on analogies. "Suppose the Paiutes chased your men off the mountains down around Delta when they went there to hunt, how would you feel?"

"But our boys know better than to hunt down there. That is Paiute country and nobody has gone there since Jake was a little boy and we got licked when we did. So we stay home and have no trouble with anybody. What does German look like? You ever see one?"

I explained that Germans look like other white people and that because of his name I was sure the agent was of German parentage.

Jake brightened up. "You tell white father we kill him for free and any other Germans that come around here too. You go fight your war. Gosiutes will stand behind you and keep Germans from capturing Ibapah valley."

It was good to know that we had such a staunch ally to fall back upon if things got real bad, but I got no place in my argument that the boys should come in and be examined.

Jake dismissed me with the promise: "We keep boys at home. Anybody come here you want killed we do it—Germans, Paiutes or Indian agents."

I reported my failure to the agent and stated that I felt the matter should be forgotten. I proceeded to do just that myself. After Charley came home from Fort Douglas I rather expected he would paint such a glowing picture of army life that the boys would go anyhow, but for once Charley kept his own counsel and took no part in the controversy.

As fall approached, I was pretty busy. I went to Ibapah every two weeks. The ducks were fat at Salt Springs. People around Wendover and the outlying settlements called the doctor for things which would never have bothered them if I had not been available. It seemed that I never was equipped for the cases which popped up. Many a time babies were born with the doctor in attendance carrying no tools of his trade except a shot gun or a fish line.

I learned to be a great improviser. One time while hunting deer in the hills above Pleasant Valley I was discovered and brought down into the valley to a man who had suffered a dislocated shoulder thirty-six hours before. The only thing I had in my car was my hypo and a roll of adhesive. I cut a hole in the bottom of the highest bunk in the bunkhouse, gave him a big hypo, put his arm through the hole and strapped a bucket of rocks to his forearm. Then I went to bed in the bunk across from him. In about an hour he let out a yell. The muscles had become relaxed, and the weight on his arm had reduced the dislocation. I got up and put his arm in a sling. We all slept the rest of the night, and I was hunting deer again at daylight. It was a rough and tumble practice and how I did enjoy it!

About Christmas Ruth discovered that a son was on the way. The Gosiute women knew it almost as soon as we did. They told Jimmy Clover to warn me not to buy a baby basket as they intended to make one for Ruth as a gift. We were a bit worried that it might be an Indian tote board, and Ruth said she would be damned if she would go back to a civilized community with her baby strapped on her back. I could not blame her for that.

The *Medical Journal* tables showed that I would be called up in March, so we tried to live every day as though it might be our last time together. The war did not seem to be going so well.

I guess the Department in Washington felt the same way, and decided to win a victory over the Gosiutes to build up the morale of the country in this anxious time. Of course I had to be in the middle again.

It was in January, 1918, I think, that the agent visited me in Gold Hill on his way back from a conference in Salt Lake City. He revealed a plan that for just plain insanity took the cake. The Indian Bureau had got tired of the Indian Rights Society badgering them and had appealed to the War Department. This in turn had bucked it on to the 20th Infantry in Fort Douglas, at Salt Lake City, with instructions to go to Ibapah, capture the tribal council, and hold them as military prisoners until the boys signed up and were inducted into the army. Here we were starting a war, in which someone might be killed, for such a trifling matter as a handful of Indians who were not covered by the draft law anyhow.

The soldiers were to come on a special train. Their advent was to be kept very quiet in order that the element of surprise might lessen the dangers of a knockout fight. My job was to wait for a code telegram which would tell the date and time of arrival. I was to secure all the cars in the valley under some pretense and have them at the train to meet the troops. And also I must come on ahead of the army and notify the agent and his women folks so that they could hightail out of there before the clambake started.

I had spent eight months trying to gain the friendship of those Indians, and now I was to repay them for their trust by doublecrossing them! Not only that, I also had to lie to my fellow townsmen to secure them and their cars, and perhaps also get them into the line of fire as drivers of the transport. This practice of medicine was putting me into one hell of a nice spot. Of one thing I was sure: If I did get back from the war and went into practice again, there would not be many problems I had not already had to meet in Gold Hill.

I spent the next few days alternating between hate for myself and a thrilling curiosity as to what was going to happen and if I could play my part without having it recorded in history as low comedy.

One morning early in February I was called to the phone and informed that grandma had died. The funeral would be five P.M. on Tuesday. The operator in Wendover who read the message to me over the railroad telephone remarked that that was a hell of a funny time for a funeral. I retorted that grandma was a hell of a funny woman.

Bright and early on Monday I started on my trip around the country to engage cars. I had to cover quite a territory to find enough to transport a hundred men. I told the ranchers a wild story about a bunch of investors arriving to look at the old Queen of Sheba mine on Ibapah, but one and all they said I must be crazy, as the snow was a foot deep. I had to promise that the road would be broken and clear for the trip. However, I had a check book in my hand and, crazy as I might be or not, money talked.

At five P.M. on Tuesday all the automobiles in the district were gathered at the depot in Gold Hill awaiting the coming of the suckers. When they began to unload, all in uniform, my friends cursed me lustily. I was not there to hear the cussing, having gone ahead to bail out that agent and his family.

The ladies also got sore at my wife. Here they were just withering on the vine because there was no Red Cross work to do but knit socks, and now there were a hundred soldier boys hungry for coffee and doughnuts and not a doughnut in the camp. Ruth was as much in the dark as the rest of them, but they were sure that she was fully informed of the plot and just held out to be snooty.

The drivers had been paid and there was nothing for them to do but load up and start for Deep Creek through the snow and sand of Gold Hill wash and the drifts that were forming on Clifton Flats.

I was some thirty miles ahead of the caravan and having my own troubles. Once I had left the valley floor the road showed an upgrade of about two hundred feet per mile. I found the snow too deep for my car to travel in high gear, and had to revert to low. To drive a Model-T Ford in low, one had to keep one's foot on the clutch pedal and press it down to the floor boards. This hindered the circulation in one's foot, which had to be kept out from under the lap robe. The night was so cold that the wheels passing through the snow crackled as though they were running over crackers. About the time I reached the last ranch, Kelly's, the radiator began to steam badly. Now both my radiator and my left foot were frozen.

It was impossible for me to travel any farther. I went into the ranch and awoke Mr. Kelly to ask his advice. Like the rest of the valley he was quite in sympathy with the Indians, but he also realized that this affair might get to be serious. He offered to saddle his horse and ride on up to the agency to warn the people there of the coming of the troops.

He insisted, however, that I should stay out in the pass and stop any Indian who might be down in Deep Creek, where he could see the cars coming down the Clifton grade and rush up to the Reservation to spread the alarm. I took his deer rifle and mounted guard out on that windswept road. The temperature on his front porch registered forty below zero. It was two o'clock in the morning, and the night was overcast and very dark.

I had been waiting and hoping all year for something romantic and dangerous to happen, and I suppose I should have been satisfied with this assignment. But I was troubled. Just suppose an Indian did come and refuse to honor my commands, what would I do then? They were my friends, and I would never think of shooting anybody whose physical welfare I was being paid to maintain. I spent a couple of hours in reflection and stamping my feet, and I wasn't very entertaining company for myself; in fact, I was pretty well disgusted at Doc Peck for getting himself into this fix.

Kelly and the agency people arrived about four o'clock. I jerked the radiator from my car and took it in behind Mrs. Kelly's stove to thaw out. Just as I was planning to do the same with my foot, Kelly called that he could see lights on Clifton mountain. We all had to go outside to look. It was a strange sight, those thirty headlights twisting and turning in the eastern sky so dark we could not see the mountain at that distance. The lights seemed to be coming out of the heavens, like an enormous glowworm descending to earth. If any Indians camped at Deep Creek did see it, they tucked their heads beneath the blankets and offered prayers to the Great Spirit, because no such cavalcade had ever been seen on that mountain at that time of night.

When the army arrived, it seemed that they were looking for me more anxiously than I was for them. To make the thing legal, the U.S. Marshal had to arrest the Indians in person, or at least read the warrant to them. The Marshal was in no shape to arrest anybody. He was a sufferer from that old man's curse, prostate enlargement. His plumbing had frozen up from riding so long in the cold, and he was in agony. The medical officers with the troops had no catheter along. If I did not have one, the whole expedition would grind to a halt. Talk about the battle being lost because of the lack of a horseshoe nail—this war almost died a-borning because of the lack of a ten cent piece of rubber tubing.

Fortunately I found one in my bag. Then the old man would not go into the house for the operation. I boiled up the catheter in the house and took him to the cattle shed where we were shielded from the wind and where, by the light of an oil lantern, I relieved him, with horses, cows and sheep as the only onlookers.

Now my hands felt frozen too. I declined their kind invitation to attend the festivities and cuddled up to Mrs. Kelly's stove. Everything thawed out but my left big toe, which was swollen for days; it still is devoid of feeling when the temperature goes below seventy.

The army marched on up the hill and within two hours marched right back down again with five frightened Indians in tow.

Those poor bucks almost smiled when they saw me. I assured them that the white soldiers meant them no harm and were not going to hang them as some joking soldier had predicted.

Kelly promised to install my auto radiator so that I could get the car next time I came by, and I joined the caravan for the trip back to Gold Hill. When we got into the valley proper, the column was stopped by Owen Sheridan, who informed us that the valley ladies had been at work since three A.M. and now had a hot breakfast ready and waiting at his ranch. The army did a left turn and descended on the Sheridan ranch like a bunch of locusts. Good old Owen himself had been doing a little preparation. He had driven over to the Nevada saloon and bought enough makings so that there was hot toddy waiting in the bunkhouse. The army called him blessed. The Indians shared in everything. Owen even got them each a blanket from his store, as the army had hurried them away about half-dressed for such weather. The world was a much more inviting-looking place as we headed into the rays of the sun just peeping over Ibapah Peak.

We arrived at Gold Hill about noon. The major in charge of the troops was all for starting right back to Salt Lake City, but he was out-maneuvered by a superior force. The Gold

Hill women were not going to be cheated out of an opportunity to feed these brave soldiers and put on a victory dance in their honor. The major knew when he was licked. The train was re-scheduled to leave the next morning.

We men got in a few naps during the day, but they were often interrupted by our wives, who insisted that we get up and do something toward making preparations for the party and dance. It was a bang-up affair—two fiddles for music, lots to eat, tubs of coffee, and plenty of rocket fuel out behind the pool hall. By midnight everybody was glad he had come.

This included the Indians. As soon as the officers had gone to bed, the guards wanted to get in on the festivities. They came over to the hall and brought their prisoners with them. Long before daylight most of the men were pretty well oiled. These soldiers were still novices in the game of war and they took their responsibilities lightly. I remember seeing the guards leaving the hall, their arms around each other's necks, singing "K-K-K-Katy" at the top of their lungs while their prisoners trailed behind carrying the guns and ammunition belts belonging to their captors.

We all went to bed pretty proud of ourselves. We had conducted a successful war, captured the enemy, and had a lot of fun. My own big toe was the only casualty. It was a campaign masterly conceived and efficiently carried out. Why should we not be proud? If the rest of the army and the civilians carried out their duties in the coming months as well as the Gold Hill contingent, the Kaiser was doomed to defeat promptly and with little fuss and confusion.

But the war was not over for me. It was a good thing I did not know it, or I would not have slept so well the few hours I tried it.

The dance broke up about two A.M., which was sort of sissyfied for Gold Hill dances, but, in view of the fact that nobody had slept any the night before, was understandable.

I was awakened at eight A.M. by someone pounding on the tent door and yelling that I was wanted immediately at the hotel. I supposed the old U.S. Marshal had suffered another plumbing failure, and grabbed my bag and hurried down there. But my professional services were not needed. As usual, I wound up doing something for which my medical training was of little use.

A report had come from Deep Creek that the remaining Indians at Ibapah Reservation had dumped the interpreter into the agency building and intended to set fire to it and roast him good before they moved down into the valley and grabbed five ranchers as hostages to insure the safe return of their tribal council which had been kidnaped by the U.S. Army.

It was a good time to have an Indian war. The army was on hand and hadn't had a chance to waste even one rifle shell, so they were invited to return to the valley and complete what they had started. But the army declined the honor with thanks. Their orders read to proceed to the Reservation and capture the five council members and retain them in custody until advised of their disposition. They had accomplished that chore and were now going home. If we natives had an uprising on our hands, it was purely our kettle of fish. Such are the wonders of the military mind in time of crisis.

After the army bowed out, the Indian agent and the U.S. Marshal held a conference and decided that because I was the only able-bodied man in town who was not seen in the raid (the others were all drivers of the cars), I was the logical man to go up to the Reservation and quell the riot. If the Indians took me hostage, I could be spared with less disruption of business than anyone else.

Another day's fee of fifty dollars plus mileage was involved. I could drive the agency car, as mine was up at

Kelly's. Since its gas tank was full, the ten cents per mile would be all gravy as well as a bit of honest graft. So why not?

I wasn't worried about my mission. I did not believe the story. The bearer of the alarming tidings was the town's leading practical joker. However, I took the precaution of calling on the prisoners to see if they had any word to send their wives and friends.

The prisoners were all in a good frame of mind and quite happy with their incarceration. Breakfast had been a big success. They had even had dried-apple pie and wished they had some money to buy some apples to send home to their wives. Their greatest want was some tobacco, but they had no money to buy any of that either. I got them a couple of dollars' worth of Bull Durham and charged it on my already shady expense account. I told them I would see them again in a couple of weeks, since they would likely be home by that time, and promised to tell their wives that they were all well. When I left, they seemed like new members of a conducted tour; they expected to see great things, eat strange food and not be bothered with the current bills.

Next I went to the general store, where a crowd was gathered, and informed the assemblage that though I was supposed to go to Ibapah to quell the riot, I would not move a step unless they contributed enough to buy a case of dried apples for me to take to the grieving wives as a peace offering. One weary husband amended the motion. He volunteered to contribute a whole dollar toward buying up the entire stock and wishing it on the Indians, regardless of the possibility that they might consider it a more direct insult to their dignity than the army raid. His only condition was that the storekeeper promise not to stock any more dried apples. That gentleman retorted that he was just as tired of dried apples as anybody else and would dispose of his stock at wholesale prices. The store cat could damned well hunt herself another place to sleep.

The stock was dumped into five large sacks—one for each lonesome widow. I had accumulated quite a nice supercargo by this time: my wife wanted to see the fun, of course; her brother showed up and offered to ride as far as Kelly's and drive my car home; and a stranger appeared who stated that he was a real live newspaper reporter for the *Salt Lake Tribune* and just had to accompany us. The possibility of being penned up in the agency as a hostage bothered him not at all. He was writing the Great American Novel anyhow, and the seclusion would give him time to get the heroine out of the mess into which he had somehow landed her.

There had been reporters for both city papers with the troops. When they left, the *Deseret News* man went with them. The *Tribune* reporter, however, had heard about my peace mission. He entered the car with his fellow craftsman and then, pretending to go to the rest room, jumped off the train after it had started. Whatever happened would now appear in the *Tribune* exclusively.

Since the dried apples filled most of the back seat, my male companions had to ride with their feet sticking out through the storm curtains. We looked more like grocery salesmen than peace emmissaries of the U.S. Government.

At the Reservation I went to the homes of the absent councilmen and left the dried apples. I am afraid my diplomatic approach was not all it should have been; the women seemed sort of sore and disgusted with the whole business. I learned afterward that they were upset because I told them that their husbands had sent the delicious fruit. Each thought she had fleeced her old man's pockets before he left to be a prisoner. If he had enough cached away to purchase all those apples, they would never trust him again. Besides he must be having a high old time and his conscience bothering him awful to be so thoughtful of his loved ones. Mamie had never enlightened me on this facet of a woman's nature—being more suspicious of her man when he tried to be thoughtful than when he came home loaded, smelling of cheap perfume, and with lipstick on his collar.

The whole camp saw me going around dispensing apples, and by the time I reached the agency most of the male population had gathered there to hear the news. I suggested that we hold a talk, and had Jimmy Clover, who was as free as anybody else, build a fire in the schoolhouse.

Once again I faced the same audience in the place of our original meeting. Annie Tommy wasn't around, however, as he had been in Idaho when the trouble started and was prudently staying there until it had all blown over. Antelope Jake was there, and so was Charley. Two friends. The rest were not so noncommittal as the first time.

I promised over and over again that the missing ones would be home as soon as the courts could rule them innocent, as they would do simply to get rid of them. Along in the afternoon Jake got up to talk. We sat in stony silence while he summed up.

"When Jake was just a baby, the white general come and tell the Gosiute fighting is wrong, you must never fight any other man. If he steal your wife or even a pony you must be good and tell the agent. If you be good Gosiutes, the government feed you; if not, you go to jail and maybe die if you kill anybody. Be peaceful always and you will be happy. Now the white soldiers come and say we must fight. They put our leaders in jail because we don't want to break our promise. You know what Jake thinks, he thinks all white men born crazy and never grow up, that's what Jake thinks."

The *Tribune* reporter disgraced himself and ran shrieking from the room and I had to cover for him by saying that my pipe had made him sick. I hadn't found anybody to pacify and we were all talked out, so I collected my party and we went home.

Two weeks later my army call had come through. I made a last trip to the Reservation to straighten out my vouchers with the agent. Charley asked me to drive down by his place, as he wanted to talk. When I got there, Jake was with him. We sat out behind the cabin and acted quite mysterious.

They did not want the agent to know that something had happened among the Indians. The council members were home again, but the boys were gone.

It seemed that a Shoshone Indian was top sergeant of the expeditionary force against the Gosiutes. He had caused more excitement among the women than Elvis would in a high-school girls' sorority. The sight of that Indian bossing all those white soldiers around was something to talk about. When the boys came in from the brush after the army left, they heard little else. They had sneaked over into Nevada and enlisted in the army, where they served well and honorably.

The Gosiutes intended to keep up the fight with the agent, however, and did not want him to feel that he had accomplished anything, as indeed he hadn't.

When I bade them goodbye, Jake suggested that, since I looked rather like an Indian myself, maybe they could hide me and I wouldn't have to go fight. He said, "Send wife home, she got blue eyes. You stay here, we fool them." I thanked him but said I wanted to go. He just put his hand to his head and made a circle with his fingers, signifying "all crazy."

Ruth was with me. She had been given that baby basket, and it was a beauty. It was made out of quarter-inch willow reeds in the shape of a clothes basket. A woven flange at the bottom kept it about a foot above the floor, and the top edge was bound in soft buckskin with buckskin handles. It was woven so tightly that it would hold water, a wise provision, as it was to be the crib of a couple of boy babies.

After them it served on our back porch as a refuge for pups, cats, rabbits, a goat and other kinds of animals that little boys are sure to bring home and want to take to bed with them.

We did not have so very much to say on our ride home. Both of us realized that this was the end of a period in our lives which we could never forget or relive.

As we drove across Clifton Flats, Ruth suggested that we drive up to our special hill—a point that commanded a view of the flat, where on sunny days the previous fall we had formed a habit of loafing a while each time we passed that way. Here we could look out over the landscape and try to imagine the time when this desolate area competed with Times Square for the title "Crossroad of the Nation." We did not talk much at these times but just sat and let the desert weave its peculiar spell around us. Today was one of those rare February days when the sun gives promise of the warmth to come. The chipmunks had come out to play, and the mountain jays were active with their nesting preparations.

We both had some thinking to do, so up we climbed and seated ourselves on the sunny side of a good-sized rock outcropping. From a remark or two I knew that Ruth was concerned with that bassinette and the individual who was going to occupy it, but I chose to review the last two years.

I thought of all the acts of kindness I had experienced which, though crude and perhaps laughable, nevertheless meant that I had acquired friendships which went deeper than just a doctor-patient relationship. Here were evidences of real friendship offered without thought of other reward than friendship returned. My sense of human values had undergone quite a change. The Gosiutes had given me lots of fun and laughter. Now I wondered if perhaps I had pre-sented the same ridiculous spectacle to them. No question about it, I was a pretty mixed-up man. It would require more than one lifetime for me properly to evaluate human behavior.

Fortunately Ruth came out of her daydream about this time. "Are we coming back to Gold Hill after you are out of the army?" she asked.

"No," I answered. "I will never again ask you to live in a house without a bathroom."

"How did you know that I so longed for a bathroom? I never complained about the lack of one, not one single time. I didn't even hint."

Without thinking, I answered, "Mamie told me."

And then there was an explosion.

"Do you mean to tell me that you asked that old hooker's advice, as well as Mrs. Gerster's, before you invited me to come out here?"

"Only in the abstract," I replied. "Mamie claimed that if a woman was forced to choose between a lifetime spent with a man without a bathroom, or a bathroom without a man, nine out of ten women would remain spinsters."

Ruth murmured, half to herself, "Thank God, I don't have to make the choice."

The evident relief of that last remark made me decide not to carry on the conversation. "Come," I said, "it's time to get back to present problems of packing. We leave tomorrow."

15

Farewell to the Desert

We sold off everything and left town with only our suitcases, the same tangible property we brought in the first place. I took Ruth to her home in central Utah, made arrangements for a most competent physician to look after her during her remaining months of waiting and the delivery of our child, and went off to help fight the war to end wars.

I didn't get very far, or contribute anything to the successful outcome. November 11, 1918, caught me sweating it out in the embarcation camp at Newport News, Virginia, waiting for a ship that never sailed.

Just when I thought I was to be released, trouble arose in the transportation of the returning wounded. The midwestern newspapers were quite bitter in condemning the army for the poor service the hospital trains were getting from the railroads. Somebody discovered my record of railroad experience, and so I was ordered to Kansas City, Missouri, where I was given the responsibility for feeding and expediting the return of wounded to hospitals over the western part of the country. Harvey's restaurant in the Kansas City Union depot and Mr. Bell, the station master, cooperated with me gladly.

Ruth would have been better off if she had stayed with the Gosiutes. A boy was delivered all right, but the second day a mix-up in the hospital resulted in his mother getting three ounces of glycerin instead of so-called tasteless castor oil. Ruth said the ensuing headache was ten times worse

than having a squaw kick you in the belly with her moc-
casined foot.

We located in Tooele, where, like the doctors before me,
I was soon so busy that I could find no time to visit my
former home in the Deep Creek Country. The Indians, however, often stopped at our house when they came through,
and we were happy to see them.

Ruth's neighbors turned up their noses and asked her
how she could stand having those dirty beggars in her
house. She just smiled and replied that those dirty beggars
had been her friends. Cleaning up any dirt they dropped
was a lot easier for her than asking them to stay outside.

I practiced medicine there for twenty-seven years. Then
when our children were grown up and through college, I
allowed my wanderlust to enter into my calculations again
and retired to a little California farm, eager to start life all
over again in an environment as strange to our way as Gold
Hill had been. "There are none happy in the world but those
who enjoy freely a vast horizon." If I might paint that lily of
a quotation, I would add the word "new" between "vast"
and "horizons."

We farmed for ten years, and then I discovered that I enjoyed farming on a typewriter. I have retired from several
occupations; I made a good living out of all of them, and
hope that there are several more yet to be experienced just
over the vast horizon. They say one should never go back,
but a few years ago when I found myself with a day to spend
in Salt Lake City, I called up a friend and we drove to
Ibapah. Nearly fifty years had gone by since I left the place,
but the valley seemed much the same until I reached the
Indian Reservation.

Where there had been nothing but sagebrush and tin cans,
now there were green alfalfa fields with plenty of good
stock grazing upon them. The wickiups were gone and each
little cabin had a radio aerial sticking up out of the roof. I

stopped at the first one and asked for some of my old friends. Most of them had gone to the happy hunting grounds, only old John Symes and his wife were living.

I had been astonished at the improvement of the surroundings, but this interview told me lots. The woman spoke excellent English, loud and clear, nothing like the deep throated grunts of her ancestors. She had to talk loud, as the radio was blaring the advantages of some new preparation to curl a lady's hair and keep it that way. Her head showed that here was one of its converts, a curly headed Indian! Shades of poor old Annie Tommy!

The Garden of Eden was being reenacted all over again. These savage Adams had lived a life of peace and inaction until their Eves heard about what sort of fig leaves the other girls were wearing. Now they were banished from this male paradise and condemned to work that their wives might follow the fashions. Hell, they were no better off than their white brothers. If progress continues, they will, I suppose, soon be suffering from stomach ulcers.

We drove over to the Symes's and found that he was away, but his daughter asked me to come in to see if her mother remembered my voice. The old lady was about ninety or a hundred years old and blind. She held my hand for a few minutes. I spoke a few words without revealing my identity. Then she rattled off a string of Gosiute to her daughter. The taboo was apparently still working among the old ladies about speaking to white men.

"She says," interpreted the daughter, " 'The young doctor has come back to us after so many years.' She says to ask you how old she is. People ask her and she is ashamed that she doesn't know. Papa tells her to wait till the white doctor comes back, he knew everything."

So through the words of this old Indian a self-confident young squirt came back to mock his aging counterpart, who over the years had discovered that what the boy had known so long ago was mostly false, and that the glamour and romance of the Old West, which he had so diligently sought, was to be found only in the imaginations of its historians.